The Law Firm REVOLUTION

Clelia Pergola   Barbara Mannino

Table of Contents

The Law Firm Revolution

Changing the mindset of law firms one lawyer at a time.

–Clelia Pergola

PREFACE

If you want something you've never had you have
to do something you've never done..

Thomas Jefferson
Part 2

If you're reading this book, you are, no doubt, a lawyer, or someone managing a firm or looking to make a difference in the firm where you work. As part of this noble club of very bright, very talented professionals, your work is governed by tremendous rules, regulations, compliance standards and ethical requirements. Combine that with your commitment to your clients in matters, often life-changing. It's fair to say, your on-the-job responsibilities are many.

Honoring all those masters can be challenging.

First, you must serve your clients. It is, no doubt, a large part of your mission is to serve your clients with the thoroughness and professionalism that leads to positive outcomes. Sometimes a resolution doesn't turn out to be what you and your client set out to accomplish. But even then, if you've managed the case with care and treated the client responsively and respect-fully, it is likely the client will come away recognizing that he's experienced superior service.

Second, you must serve the Law. You are bound to certain standards—both practices that have been legislated and others that are tied to honoring rules and ethics. The specter of malpractice is forever a back drop for your initiatives. And to circumvent the attention to that master compromises service to your client.

Finally, you must serve those around you: your partners, paralegals and administrative staff. They are there to assist you with the tasks that are necessary to completion of case work yet, in the case of your administra-tive staff, outside the scope of strictly legal matters and the practice of law. You must rely on them to perform to their maximum capability and then some. But for them to perform at that high level, you must treat them with respect and make them understand that their work and contributions are valued and that they are an integral part of your team.

It's tough to manage all these masters, and the pressure to do so can get you into the weeds. You take on everything and do too much, particularly when it comes to the administrative, nonlegal tasks such as marketing, reviews, reports, court customer service, etc.. Lawyers, particularly those in small or solo firms, have been doing this for years. Their result: stacks of paper-work piled high in their offices, long hours at work, and, in worst case sce-narios, a growing list of dissatisfied clients who are critical of their lawyer's lack of responsiveness. As troubling, the scenario translates to the absence of work/life balance, undue stress on families and personal lives that suffer. In fact, it has been said, that because they feel burdened and overwhelmed with their work, lawyers often come across as an unhappy lot.

But today, innovative ideas and the evolution of technology tools are available as phenomenal aids that can help you develop processes, nurture people and maximize technology. This book identifies many of the key ideas that will improve your practice management and make your workdays more productive.

That's not to say you'll never encounter bumps in the road. But when you do, you will recognize that you have the knowledge to accept them, learn from them and address them to grow your practice and further your professional development.

And, best of all, because of the more effective and efficient way you'll be managing your practice, you may even recapture the passion that set you on this rewarding and important career path in the first place.

It's never too late…

ABOUT THE AUTHORS

Clelia Pergola has spent most of her career in the legal profession, most recently as the Co-Founder and Chief Operating Officer of Goldberg Law Group. The organization and the people, processes and technologies that support it have been a constant focus for her throughout her career, and her colleagues attest that she is the force behind Goldberg Law's rapid growth. From pricing, to business development to bringing the firm's mission, vision and values to life, Clelia has provided inspirational leadership and modeled the intractability it takes to stand up to challenges and facilitate business growth. Her success at Goldberg Law and her continuous desire to help others have motivated her to found Lexfirma Consulting, in which she helps attorneys adopt the best practices that will help them develop professionally and successfully shepherd their firms' growth. *The Law Firm Revolution* is yet another way she can help others achieve and succeed. As CEO of the ElderPro Network, a networking resource for professionals in the eldercare industry, Clelia delivered on a personal mission to be a resource for caregivers, particularly working women. In this role, she extended her caregiving role for her beloved Nonna and Nonno, who taught her the importance of caring and family from the time she was a child, to help others navigate the eldercare environment when they face challenging times. Her role on the home front as a devoted wife and mom to husband, Brandon, and their two boys, Dante Domenico and Gino Angelo, have deepened the integrity and passion with which she approaches her work. Clelia's capacity to link the science of operational management with the soft skills of thoughtful, compassionate leadership well position her to share her ideas and methodologies to help others learn and grow.

Barbara Mannino is a freelance journalist who has spent her career in the newsroom. She has written for Fox Business Network, entrepreneur.com and ghostwritten articles for others that have appeared on Huffington Post. Her work has also been published in many financial services publications. She has written extensively on leadership and workplace issues in organizations cross industry, including the law. Her work reflects her understanding of the way soft skills that include communication, compassion and the ability to foster relationships complement functional expertise to form a powerful combination for leadership. The *Law Firm Revolution* is yet another example of that. Barbara is recognized by sources and clients as a professional who researches thoroughly, interviews thoughtfully and listens attentively before she even picks up her pen. Her work has raised awareness, struck a chord and inspired action in others. She is known for her unbiased and fair reporting. Those who have worked with Barbara describe her as a journalist who truly role models the balance of results and relationships as she works to make a human connection with the people she interviews, all the while maintaining the integrity of her story.

FOREWORD

Almost seven years ago a young woman was hired as part-time receptionist at the law firm where I then worked. That moment in itself wasn't especially auspicious—a new receptionist accepting a job seemingly in order to pay the bills with plans to move on when another short-term opportunity arose. I wasn't aware at the time, though, how powerful this individual was and how her intuitive ability to break down large concepts into their simplest form would eventually catapult her career (and mine) into something bearing absolutely no resemblance to its original trajectory.

Clelia Pergola is headstrong, opinionated, and dogged in her pursuit to complete tasks and teach others, an art that comes to her naturally. One could spend years educating herself in the tenets of business and never attain Clelia's intuitive ability to take creative ideas and immediately transform them into business concepts complete with a step-by-step road map. Her processes have enabled us to handle an ever-growing client base of satisfied seniors and their families. Through Clelia's guidance, Goldberg Law Group has become well known for its ability to solve complex problems in a fast, efficient and friendly manner.

Clelia and I met Barbara Mannino when the three of us were part of an organization offering services and support to seniors and their families and caregivers. Barbara, who was the content writer for the group, is a well-respected journalist who draws on her writing and reporting background to help businesses and organizations recognize the characteristics that comprise effective leadership and, in this process, develop content to promote their brands.

Aging and longevity can be a very sensitive subject, but Clelia and I observed how insightful Barbara was in offering ideas, thorough she was in researching material and asking important questions, and skilled she was in writing strong, but sensitive, prose that resonated with our audience. Importantly, Barbara demonstrated an enthusiasm for the diverse subject matter to which she was exposed in this group, whether law, finance, real estate or health, and this always resonated in her story.

For these reasons, I was very pleased to learn that Clelia had reached out to Barbara and asked her to co-author this book.

In *The Law Firm Revolution*, Clelia and Barbara cover all the key strategies and tactics that comprise effective practice management. I can attest to this because by following the rules outlined in their book, we at Goldberg Law are able to spend quality time with our families, our clients, and our professional resources, and build a cohesive team of professionals who enjoy working together—all while serving our clients in a dynamic and resourceful style.

Clelia and Barbara have collaborated to use their research and experience to tell a comprehensive story that will help lawyers, individuals managing a firm or staff members who want to make a difference how to enrich a firm's culture, enhance its practice management, facilitate its growth and further the professional development and reputations of a firm's lawyers and the indispensable people who work with them.

For those professionals who wish to concentrate on their chosen field and stop being bogged down in managerial minutia to service clients clearly and efficiently and build their firms into a solid practice, this book is for you.

Eric Goldberg
Cofounder and
Principal Attorney
Goldberg Law Group

PART I:

If You Build It, They Will Come

CHAPTER 1

The Dilemma

Growth is never by mere chance;
it is the result of forces working together.

- James Cash
Founder of JC Penney

Getting the Right People

Before you even get to the brick and mortar aspect of your practice or the clients who will help you build revenue, you must zero in on the people who will be working with you behind the scenes. People are at the heart of any law practice and any business, and the biggest issue for any company tends to be around building your team. It's your most important predictor of success. but how do you know you'll select the right people and build the right team?

There are absolutely no winners in a situation in which the wrong person is hired for a job opening, perhaps because the need to fill the position at last or quickly overrides a careful search. Most managing partners, employers and employees can share the horror stories of being on one end or the other of this disastrous situation. Typically, there's little trust on the part of an employer that the employee will perform to expectations. The employee, in turn, is uninspired and disengaged; there is typically awkwardness and timidity of what to do and how to do it, and the sense that his or her work won't be appreciated. Passive aggressiveness often becomes a companion behavior and behind-the-back divisive gossip becomes the team MO.

Spend the time

A thorough candidate selection process can prevent situations like this from occurring. Plus, it definitely pays dividends long-term.. Spend the time. Even if this means you spend more time recruiting than you'd like, an off-the-cuff recruitment process and uninspired interviewing won't do. Recruitment without retention will end up costing you more money in the long run. Plus, you'll waste time, and productivity will lag, too. Investing your time and money in people who have the right attitude and the skill set and accomplishments for the position you need to fill requires will pay off immensely down the road.

Unique yet interdependent

Think of each team member as having a unique talent that brings value to a larger whole. Their specific talents are not duplicative but interdependent. A Super Bowl team can't have three quarterbacks on the field at one time, but a quarterback, a fullback, a tight end and wide receiver are among the teammates who pull together on each offensive play to successfully pass and run the ball down the field.

Taking flight with DISC

Therefore, it's not just about any one person. It's about everyone on the team and their relationships with each other. When you really think about it, successful relationships are what good teams are all about.

Then why is it that some teams work in harmony, while others are always at odds and have little to show for their work? There are, of course, many reasons for this, but one of the main factors is the interplay of the different behavioral styles of team members. Diversity may be the key to success in team-building. But, realistically speaking, put all those diverse personalities with their individual work styles together without a good grasp of how they'll mesh; you could be putting out fires on a regular basis.

That's why making a concerted effort to cultivate mutually supportive relationships between team members goes a long way to ensuring the team performs effectively. And, DISC, a personality profiling tool, can facilitate this and provide a useful predictor of team effectiveness. In fact, understanding the personality styles defined by DISC—even requiring candidates to participate in a DISC personality test—helps an employer get a better understanding during the recruitment process of whether a candidate will mesh with existing team members and, then, when onboarding a new employee, inject some personalization into the process.

DISC gives you as a managing partner and employer the tools to manage diverse personalities; as a staff member, it gives you an opportunity to be more self-aware of your behaviors in specific situations, even field curve balls when they're thrown at you. By identifying patterns of behavior and a set of personal traits, you cannot only better predict how individual team members will react to a situation but also identify the issues that can occur when diverse types work together. What's more, DISC can suggest ways of attacking problem areas—even better, head them off at the pass by providing insight on how to manage diverse personalities to create the solidarity of your team.

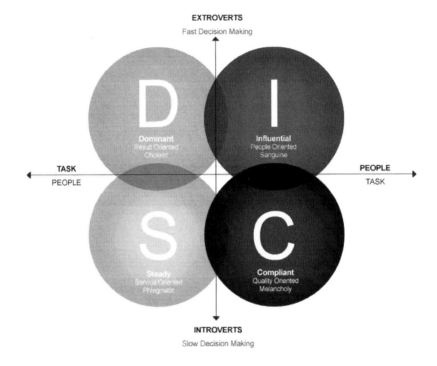

Courtesy Google Images

DISC identifies four personality styles, and the parts they play in the development and performance of the team.

♦ **Dominant.** This personality style is particularly suited to a leadership role within a team. Dominant team members are risk-takers, problem solvers and decision makers. They focus on the big picture, and have innovative ideas. The number of highly dominant team-members on a team should be kept to a minimum. Because they tend to be authoritative, they do not always listen to the ideas of others. Several people attempting to take a leadership role within a team will clearly have a negative impact on team performance.

♦ **Influential.** The influential personality style is the glue that holds the team together. Unless influential team members possess specialized skills, they often appear to have little practical influence on a team's proceedings, and, as a result, are often undervalued. Still, an effectively working team is dependent on its members feeling they are a cohesive unit, and one or two influential team members can foster this esprit de corps. Influencers are also generally communicative and comfortably fill the role of the team spokesperson who presents the team's ideas and findings to others.

♦ **Steady.** Steady team members are reliable and dependable. They focus on harmony and are quick to encourage their work peers to avoid quick judgements and actions that compromise the collegiality and the efficient operations of the team. They are good listeners and patient with others, traits that work well when the team has gelled and is either brainstorming ideas or moving ahead to complete projects. The S's are great multitaskers and persistent in seeing tasks and projects through to completion. They are loyal to their teams but need to feel their environment is safe before they render an opinion, give feedback or speak out.

♦ **Compliant.** Compliant team members like structure and precision and are detail oriented and results driven. Those members with high compliance scores will tend to be the ones who generate ideas and produce materials and reports and often possess the specialized skills and knowledge conducive to project completion. Interestingly, they share some of the control preferences of the dominant personality style, but because they are nonassertive, they exercise control through their attachment to rules and codes of behavioral conduct rather than giving direction to others on their team.

Teams don't just operate effectively on Day 1. In fact, like people, teams experience growing pains and actually must go through fluctuations early on before they begin to perform effectively. During this formative period, relationships and roles within the group are formed and take hold. This formative period is an ideal time to introduce any formal structures that will help the group operate smoothly and cohesively.

Indispensable or Irreplaceable...which is which

A successful person once asked us if anyone on our respective teams was indispensable. We had to think about that long and hard. As we're writing this, we each have a team whose MO is pretty smooth; yet is anyone truly indispensable?

Some people mistake indispensable for irreplaceable, says Amy Hoover, president of Talent Zoo, "but they're not the same thing." As they say, everyone can be replaced. But to be indispensable means that you are so good and efficient at your job, that your boss and coworkers don't want to imagine replacing you," she says. "You are the go-to person they count on; the one who simply gets things done."

With Amy's disclaimer in mind, we dug a little further and found this list of ten traits in the *PM Times*, a resource for project managers, which lists those traits which collectively describe employees who are considered indispensable team members. These employees:

- ♦ Participate fully
- ♦ Speak truthfully
- ♦ Act reliably
- ♦ Maintain a positive attitude
- ♦ Focus on solutions

- Practice being proactive

- Share knowledge

- Demonstrate personal initiative

- Practice continuous improvement

- Promote team success

Team members who are tenacious and diligent in demonstrating these behaviors serve as outstanding role models for other members. Typically, most employees want to perform well and support their team's success. And, if they are self-aware, they'll want to adopt situation-appropriate mannerisms, emulate behaviors that will help the team and, in the process, make themselves look good.

Owners, partners and managers can more easily trust employees who function in an exemplary way and consistently count on them to get their assigned tasks completed correctly. Knowing you can trust your team enables you to give more focus to your work.

Chapter To-Do's and Takeaways
Here are some ideas to select and nurture individuals to support a strong team:

Recruit purposefully

The road to employee retention requires a well-thought out, purposeful search process, explains Andrew LaCivita in *The Hiring Prophecies*. As founder and chief executive officer of milewalk, a Chicago-based recruitment firm, LaCivita used milewalk's 10-year study to predict recruitment and retention success. So dig deep. While you must pay attention to a candidate's functional requirements and his/her relevant accomplishments, look at his/her capacity to stretch and risk trying new things—even his/

her ability to risk failure. Plus, you can't overlook their emotional intelligence. Humans have the empathy and the ability to understand others. We can learn to be good communicators and to speak with clarity, persuasion and respect. If you're interviewing prospects at this deep level, you will be able to gather this pertinent information. Many experts also recommend the DISC criteria to set the standard for the traits you need in your team.

Set goals and make sure they're realistic

Setting short and long-term goals with your team becomes the foundation for daily tasks as well as for reinforcing the big picture. Help them understand that the work they perform every day aligns with your firm's mission and vision and supports the values you all have agreed upon for your firm. People need and want to believe that what they are doing has relevance. Deadlines and the milestones that result from them give your staff members opportunities to help each other out and band together for success. At Goldberg Law, we set time aside at the beginning of each year for the team to work together on vision boards. We ask them to use illustrative examples of the goals they have set for themselves individually as well as the goals they've been tasked with by our management team. Capturing the goals in this way brings them to life and deepens their commitment to them.

Celebrate successes

Celebrating milestones makes your team feel valued and goes to show that when they work together, great things can happen. When team members do a terrific job, make sure their efforts are acknowledged and appreciated, and describe why. Give them a public shout out. The recognition will help them feel what they're doing has value and impact.

Accept failures

In contrast, if your team fails at something, come together to redirect your efforts or turn it into something positive. Don't throw anyone under the bus or turn a damage-control discussion into a blame game. This never helps anybody. Instead, call a team meeting and together figure out the next steps or course corrections. Help staff members learn by discussing what they might do the next time they are faced with a similar situation.

Getting to know you

You are, of course, never obligated to become best friends on a personal level with your team members, nor should you. But having a monthly outing or engaging in some offsite socializing quarterly can give employees a chance to appreciate one another beyond the daily grind and may well help diffuse stressful interactions with them when work days get tough. These kindnesses will leave them with a lasting impression of your softer, human side, and serve to dispel their anxiety when things go wrong. What's more, the interest you put in their overall well-being is a definite retention builder that will keep them longer at your firm.

Spread the word

We're taught to back up our data, but generally we are not as focused on backing up our employees. Your people are among your firm's most valuable assets. Still, as we've said, it is not wise to consider even the most indispensable employee as irreplaceable. Why risk being caught short? Give each team member a secondary role so that he or she is trained to understand the requirements of a colleague's primary role. The secondary person has the knowledge of another role as needed and, essentially, he or she is on call, even to help when a colleague needs assistance because he's overloaded with work.

CHAPTER 2

What's Your Purpose?

You've got to think about big things while you're doing small things so that all the small things go in the right direction.

-*Alvin Toffler*
American Writer & Futurist

Like people, businesses need a sense of purpose. Law firms are no different.

In business, purpose, in its simplest form, is an organization's reason for being. It's what gave you as the founder of a law firm the motivation to start your practice. And, as a lawyer, paralegal or staff member, it's that sense of what drives the law firm—the purpose that should be embedded in its culture. It's what attracted you to the firm.

Let's call this the emotional component behind the organization—the soft piece, the glue that holds an organization together and creates a direction for your practice, what your overall strategy is, who you serve, how you operate. If you want to create a direction for the future of your practice, and a way of doing business that inspires you, your entire firm, and your clients, creating vision and mission statements are a good place to start. Once you have a clear direction, making real progress toward your goals is much easier, and reduces that feeling of being overwhelmed. Vision, mission and values are the first step toward creating the practice that you want. Establish them, write them down and share them with everyone who works on your team. Inspire them and make their work more than a daily grind but instead something in which they can believe.

The problem is that lawyers, particularly those in small firms or lawyers tasked with managing their practices, are operating without a clear sense of purpose. They have no real business plan, no clear sense of why their clients come to them for services, what their clients do and don't like about the firm and where the revenue and profitability come from. Don't worry if you fall into this category. It is only natural that you become consumed in the everyday activities of the firm, tend to feel overwhelmed by the case load with its paperwork and phone calls and just go about your day-to-day operations—working hard, yes, but often aimlessly and without direction with little idea about how to build your firm, bring in more profitable work and better clients, even diversify the practice

The fact is: Whether you're starting a new firm or already engaged in an existing one, taking the time to think through, discuss, and establish a vision and mission and the accompanying values for the firm is both a good starting point or the perfect opportunity to get on course. Having a compelling idea (vision) of what you want to achieve in the future, and a clear understanding of what you are doing now (mission) to achieve that vision is the most important foundational tool for goal setting and planning. Vision and mission are also at the core of your firm's values, which establish the manner in which you go about providing services to your clients.

To paraphrase Michael Gerber, author of *The EMyth Revisited*, this is the time to start working ON your firm not IN it. By crafting your vision and mission statements, you are creating the touchstones for everything you undertake, from strategic planning, marketing, management and practice building to recruitment, hiring and performance evaluations. These two statements are important, concrete guides for the future of your practice. Once the vision and mission are written and digested, the rest of your business activities, including the management and marketing of your practice, have a direction and will begin to fall more easily into place.

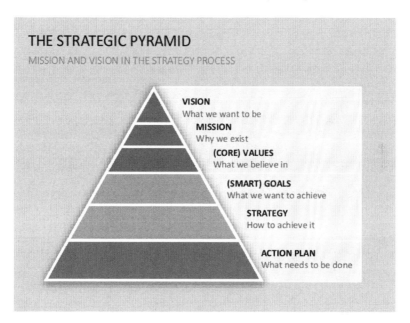

Courtesy Google Images

Some definitions:

Vision statement:

Your vision statement will tell a compelling story about the future you are going to create. Some experts recommend your vision statement is a forward look of three to five years, others advocate for a longer-term view, perhaps as many as 10. But because innovation is causing the marketplace to change at almost the speed of light today, the shorter time frame may work better for your firm.

A vision statement describes the organization as it would appear in a future successful state. When developing a vision statement, try to answer this question: If the organization were to achieve all its strategic goals, what would it look like maybe even 10 years from now? An effective vision statement is inspirational and aspirational. It creates a mental image of the future state that the organization wishes to achieve. A vision statement should challenge and inspire employees.

Mission Statement:

After you have come up with your vision statement the next step is to summarize what you are doing in the present and identify just who your clients are. Your mission statement, then, summarizes the work you do, the clients you do it for, and the characteristics that distinguish your firm from your competitors.

What's more, that uniqueness can't be emphasized enough. To be effective, the mission statement should be unique to you and set you apart. It must reflect your personality, as the founder of the firm, and the collective personality of the people who work there.

A mission statement explains your firm's reason for existence. It describes what it does and its overall intention. The mission statement supports the vision and serves to communicate purpose and direction to employees, customers, vendors and other stakeholders.

The mission can change to reflect a company's priorities and methods to accomplish its vision.

Values

Once you have established your vision and mission, it's time to talk values. Values describe the core beliefs intrinsic to your firm. Values are the heart of your culture and the foundation of all the actions and investments you will make.

Your vision, mission, and values form the foundation of your firm's plan and are the foundational tools for setting your short and long term goals.

It's not about you

A note to those of you who already do have vision and mission statements: It's important to take the time to make sure your existing statements pass the litmus test.

Many law firm mission statements focus on the firm or lawyer—their education, their skills, etc. They neglect to touch on the target audience and the problems, issues and goals important to the people in that target audience. In fact, the mission statement must focus on your prospective clients and how you and your firm will help find solutions to their problems. It should also include how you meet client needs better than or in a different manner than your competitors do. It's not about you. It's about your clients and how you can be of service to them.

And, for whom and for what...

When creating vision, mission and values, it's also important to understand whom they serve—who the stakeholders are. These statements comprise the common ground for all stakeholders: your firm's founding partners, your staff, other professionals and organizations with whom and with which you do business, and for your clients who need to have expectations of how you will serve them.

To make sure everyone is aware of your firm's vision, mission and value statements, they must be visible, widely circulated and discussed often so that their meaning is understood, shared, and internalized. This means that they should appear on your website which is your face to the outside world, and they should be referenced in team meetings, in-service sessions or firm retreats. What better way for employees to understand what is expected of them, know how best they can serve your firm and its clients, understand the firm's strategy and implementation and keep them focused on how they can create value for your firm?

Also, remember vision statement, a mission statement and the values statements have their own distinct function in the strategic planning process and assist you in crafting a roadmap for strategy development. In fact, one measure of the effectiveness of your strategy is answering the question of how well that strategy helps the firm achieve its goals as stated in the vision and mission.

Our own research has led us to this description of the relationship among vision, mission and strategy: visualize them collectively as a funnel. At the broadest part of the funnel, you find the inputs into the mission statement. Toward the narrower part of the funnel, you find the vision statement, which has distilled down the mission to guide the development of the strategy. In the narrowest part of the funnel you find the strategy—it is clear and explicit about what the firm will do, and not do, to achieve the vision.

Vision statements also provide a bridge between the mission and the strategy. According to London Business School professors Gary Hamel and C. K. Prahalad, the best vision statements create a tension and restlessness regarding the status quo—that is, they should foster a spirit of continuous innovation and improvement and describe this tense relationship between vision and strategy as stretch and ambition. In a study of competitors such as CNN, British Airways, and Sony, Hamel and Prahalad found that these firms displaced competitors with stronger reputations and deeper pockets through their ambition to stretch their organizations in more innovative ways

Vision and mission provide a high-level guide, and the strategy provides a specific guide, to the goals and objectives showing success, failure or progress to goal of the strategy and satisfaction of the larger set of objectives stated in the mission.

For its part, your firm's values statement describes what your firm believes in and how it will behave. In a values-led firm, the values create a moral compass for the company and its employees and guide decision-making and establish a standard against which actions can be assessed. A values statement defines the deeply held beliefs and principles of the organizational culture. These core values are an internalized framework that is shared, acted on and modeled by leadership. Not all organizations create or are able to uphold a values statement, so keep in mind, if your firm can, it benefits from yet another mechanism to keep its operation on course.

Your founding partners cannot create a new values statement and expect the values to simply become core values. For the organization to have an effective values statement, it must fully embrace its values and use them to guide its attitudes, actions and decision-making every day. According to the Society for Human Resources Management, developing a values-led organization can be a difficult and slow process that should be attempted only by organizations that are willing and prepared to make a long-term commitment to the established company values.

Chapter To-Do's and Takeaways

Your vision, mission and values are the heart and soul of your business.

By crafting your vision and mission statements, you are creating the touchstones for everything you undertake.

Admittedly, figuring out these more philosophical aspects of your business, even more so, memorializing them in writing, can seem like an insurmountable task, creating a barrier that prevents you from doing it. Still, the importance of completing this task cannot be underestimated.

Some Tools to Get You Started

We've adapted these questions from Matthew Cleek and Entrepreneur Media to law firms to help you formulate your statements and get you on your way.

Answer these questions in writing:

Vision

1. What problem does my organization seek to solve?

2. Why do I believe this problem needs to be addressed?

3. Does this problem matter to other people?

4. Do I honestly believe we have the answer to that problem? (elaborate)

5. What changes do I believe my organization can affect?

6. What are the greatest strengths of my organization?

7. What is my dream for this organization?

8. How would things be different if my dream came true?

9. Does my dream connect on a personal level with others?

Use your written answers to craft your statement based on a statement that defines where you want your firm to be in five years. Having been down this road with clients on many occasions, we advise that you adopt the following mindset: this will only be your first draft. These statements take time and tweaking. Revisit it, test your self-awareness, ask yourself whether you're being realistic and honest with yourself. Consider whether the statement is inspirational. Even share it with others to get their reaction. You'll know when you've gotten it right.

Now it's time to write your mission statement. Entrepreneur Media suggests some questions to get you started and we've adapted them here for law firms:

Mission

1. **Why are you practicing law?** What do you want for yourself, your family and your clients? Think about the spark that ignited your decision to become a lawyer. What will keep it burning?

2. **Who are your clients?** What can you do for them that will provide solutions to their problems, give them direction for the future, enrich their lives and contribute to their success—now and in the future?

3. **What image of your firm do you want to convey?** Clients, competitors and other professionals will have perceptions of your company. How will you create the desired picture and live up to their expectations?

4. What is the nature of your services and practice areas? What factors determine pricing and quality? Consider how these relate to the reasons for your firm's existence. How will all this change over time, say if you grow your firm or diversify your practice?

5. What level of service do you provide? Most firms believe they offer "the best service available," but do your clients and the outside world agree? Don't be vague; define what differentiates your service from your competitors.

6. What roles do you and your employees play? Wise captains develop a leadership style that organizes, challenges and recognizes employees. How does this help your firm operate more efficiently?

7. What kind of relationships will you maintain with other professionals and organizations whose businesses and services are complementary to your business? Every business is in partnership with its suppliers. When you succeed, so do they.

8. How do you differ from competitors? Many entrepreneurs forget they›re pursuing the same dollars as their competitors. What do you do better, cheaper or faster than competitors? How can you use competitors' weaknesses to your advantage?

9. How will you use technology, capital, processes, and services to reach your goals? A description of your strategy will keep your energies focused on your goals.

10. What underlying philosophies or values guided your responses to the previous questions? Some businesses choose to list these separately. Writing them down clarifies the "why" behind your mission.

To arrive at a set of values, ask yourself some questions:

1. What standards do we want everyone to follow when they make decisions?

2. What behaviors do we want stakeholders to model?

3. How do we approach solving the most difficult problems?

4. What do we want others to understand about our firm from watching our behavior?

5. What kinds of activities exemplify what we value most?

6. What do we want our staff to say about how they were treated by us?

7. What do we want those served by our organization to say about their experience with us?

8. What is our desired reputation in the marketplace?

9. What makes us grateful? What makes us happy when we are at work?

Now you're ready to put it all together. Here are some helpful tips.

It takes a village. Poll colleagues, if you have them, or friends and other professionals. Ask them to rate the power of your words for inspiration, motivation, etc., and call out any gaps. Choose supportive people who care about your success.

Take the time. Writing short, tight and to the point takes time…lots of time. Allocate at least a day to initially accomplish this task. Then step away and review your words, taking more time to edit. The time you spend will shine through in your finished product.

Mark your calendar. Set up a meeting with the people who will be helping you put your thoughts on paper. Make sure you meet behind closed doors so there are no distractions.

Begin at the beginning. Thoroughly explain mission, vision and values—what they are and why they're important to your firm. Not everyone will automatically recognize that they are as important to small firms as they are to large corporations.

Discount nothing. There's no idea too crazy or silly to get you started. That's what gets the juices flowing. Run the foundational questions by them and use a white board or flip chart to record their reactions. When you've finished gathering ideas, ask everyone to write out some statements for your firm. Read them aloud, and much like working on a puzzle, combine the best pieces and meld them into a meaningful whole.

Words matter. Once you have your ideas down pat, experiment with the word choices that will make your ideas pop off the page. Your statement should call forth mental images and have sensory appeal to create a connection with professionals, peers and prospects.

PART II

Systems and Processes are Everything

CHAPTER 3

Cut Through the Fog

Obstacles are those frightful things you see when
you take your eyes off your goal.

–Henry Ford
Founder of the Ford
Motor Company

Now that you've gotten past what you think might be the hard stuff—the more philosophical vision, mission and values—it's time to take those high-level inspirational concepts and translate them into some hard core strategic planning.

Strategic planning lays out goals for the long-term and, also, as importantly, for the short-term. Long-term goals really are actionable translations of your vision and mission. Short-term goals are those goals you want to accomplish in say three months, six months, at the most ,a year. They are smaller subsets of your long-term goals, and they're concrete, more readily attainable, but with a bit of stretch, and they define measurable objectives. Their attainability and their ability to be easily measurable are essential as a base for evaluating your progress, both in terms of your execution of specific short-term objectives and your determination of how specific short-term objectives measures up to your long-term goals.

One important thing to remember: short-term goals build incrementally toward the achievement of your long-term goals. Without them, your big picture plan will never be implemented.

That's why we can't emphasize enough the importance of strategic planning. Along with vision and mission, it's one of your first foundational actions and an ongoing imperative as you establish your long-term goals and establish and execute the short-term objectives that will help you achieve them.

Always a work in progress

Key to this thinking is understanding that your practice is always a work in progress. Market needs change, client needs change, you may change and expand or contract your practice focus, and you must be flexible and agile enough to adapt to any of these changes by editing your short-term performance objectives.

A law firm, or any organization for that matter, without a plan is like a ship adrift at sea in the fog. Therefore, your strategic planning is never really done. You are always course correcting and righting the ship. It's never too late to get started and never a waste of time to review your plan regularly and tweak as necessary. In fact, these actions are absolutely imperative if you want your practice to flourish.

Your firm can be hugely successful if you consistently set short-term, attainable goals. The first step is identifying those goals. The second step is outlining the necessary steps to reach them. The third step is backing them up with realistic, thoroughly researched quantifiable benchmarks for evaluating performance outcomes.

So, what do you want to accomplish this quarter, this half year or this year, and what objectives are most important for the forward movement and growth of your firm? And, then, how do you want to deliver on these objectives?

Here are some possibilities to consider:

- ▶ **Communicate continuously.** This is an important goal which merits its own discussion as you will see in Chapter 8. Your staff plays a vital role in your practice. These are the folks who are in the trenches, typically the people who onboard new clients, assign a specific client case to the right attorney, and/or field questions and calls daily from clients.

- ▶ **Amp up your marketing.** There are several avenues through which you can accomplish this goal. For example, you might consider starting a blog for your practice and follow up by making regular postings on a weekly, monthly or other established basis. You or one of your colleagues could write this and publish the blog via your website. Also remember to periodically review your website to make certain it accurately portrays you, your colleagues and your firm, and, as importantly, speaks to the needs of your customers.

- ▶ **Up your networking ante.** Research shows that lawyers typically don't like to network, engage in marketing activities and cultivate new business. But these activities are imperatives for law firms, or any business today, and there are several ways to accomplish this. For example, sponsor an event. At our firm, we hold a monthly cocktail hour and invite business contacts and ask them to bring along their friends and professional contacts. This creates opportunities to build relationships and develop trust among professionals whose clients may have needs for our services as well as theirs, and generally increases our opportunity to create strategic partnerships and build out our referral base. You or your colleagues might also join professional networking organizations. Capitalize on these activities by setting target goals for colleagues to engage in one-to-one meetings with prospects and other professionals. There is nothing better than a face-to-face meeting to build a relationship.

▶ **Respond quickly.** We cover this in depth in Chapter 7, but getting back to clients in a timely fashion and with a meaningful response can mean the difference between satisfied and dissatisfied clients. Your client satisfaction quotient cannot be underestimated. Your firm's reputation is riding on it.

▶ **Streamline and simplify.** Automating certain functions and developing processes that streamline the way both your lawyers and staff accomplish daily activities will improve efficiency and result in less stress for everyone. Better systems and processes will also improve task completion, facilitate better turnaround time for client service and result in clients who will happily provide word-of-mouth referrals to their friends, business associates and other prospects.

Wildly important goals

Admittedly, there are many short-term goals to choose from. But here's an important point: narrow your focus to one or two wildly important goals

(WIGs) and consistently invest your team's time and energy into them. According to Chris McChesney, Sean Covey and Jim Huling in their book *The 4 Disciplines of Execution,* if you want high-focus, high-performance team members and a high-performance practice, you all must have something wildly important to focus on. No team can focus on more than two WIGs at the same time.

A word about execution

Implicit in this concept of short term goals is execution. Back track for a moment to the creation of your vision and mission and your core beliefs, then your creation of a strategic plan. As sound as they may be, if you don't follow through and deliver on the plan—if you tuck that five-page typewritten plan into your top desk drawer and fail to look at it again—you've got nothing…literally nothing. You've got to execute to leverage success, accept and tweak failure and move your practice forward, and in a law firm or in any business, execution is little more than a set of behaviors that get you from point A to point B. It's no different than a goal to be thinner (high-level goal), to lose 10 pounds in two months (short-term goal) with an execution to walk two miles each morning and a reduced caloric intake (the behavior that gets you to your desired outcome).

Law firms that succeed in building their practices not only have a plan, but also the partners, likely with some employee input, have an agreed upon set of best practices—e.g., best behaviors—in place against which they can execute. They also have a measurement for accountability to ensure that the plan and the best practices are executed.

And one additional perspective: You will experience success with some of your objectives; with others, you may not. But if you've done everything possible in your execution to make it work, you must never be afraid or ashamed to fail. The key is to leverage your success and learn from your failure.

To leverage or learn

But how will you know just how well you have or haven't done? Unless you're bringing in tons of profit, or, on the other hand, are calamitously working to barely make ends meet, how can you really get a handle on how well you're doing?

You really can't, unless, of course, you measure. Without measurement, you'll just go along, performing your daily activities as you think you should or as you have been doing and your ultimate success or failure will most probably be at the whim of chance. What's more, because your course is undirected and without evaluation, you may likely feel overwhelmed and stuck in the weeds. But if you track your results, you can evaluate your execution and leverage your successes or figure out why your outcomes either fell short of your expectations, even worse, failed miserably. Learn from your analysis and course correct and move forward.

The nuts and bolts of the strategic planning process are expressed in measurable goals. Measurable goals set specific, concrete objectives, which means they're expressed in terms of tangible quantities (percentages and dollars and cents in terms of increasing revenue and equate that to a correspondent increase in the number of clients you'll need) and timelines (by when do you want to accomplish a certain goal). This becomes clearer when comparing the difference in these two statements: "To grow substantially during the next few years" versus "to increase revenue by 30 percent and 15 more clients during the upcoming year." The first sentence is far too general to be a short-term goal, but the second nails exactly what must be done.

By providing a concrete example, the second sentence provides a tangible objective and a time frame in which to complete it. That's important because that measurable goal enables you to evaluate your progress and determine if the target date is realistic. If it is, you're pacing your objective correctly; if it isn't, you need to tweak the time frame. It also enables you to determine whether the 30 percent 15 client calculation is realistic or whether that requires adjustment. The key here is analyzing sufficiently to make the edit, not to feel failed. Even if you don't accomplish your objective in the originally allotted time frame, even if you don't achieve all your objectives, the act of planning in and of itself is a milestone that can improve your focus, give you clarity, and renew your motivation and commitment to the success of your firm.

The best of short-term planning

This type of strategic plan with its emphasis on the role short-term planning plays has several advantages. It can help you assess your market, plan a correspondent course of action and develop specific behavior strategies to help you achieve desired outcomes. In large part, these strategies will be focused on improving the methods you use to complete tasks and the measures you can take to grow your business,. As a result, they will be directed toward marketing and networking activities as well as on the efficiency of your practice operations and the embedding of a can-do/will-do attitude in the culture of your firm.

And, while marketing is typically not in an attorney's skill set, it is nonetheless an essential part of the action steps you must take to grow your business. Part of your short-term plan, then, might be calling in a marketing expert to help you with some of the activities you will require to market your firm.

Plus, having a plan will put you in a better position to allocate funds for these endeavors.

At the same time, having a plan and the resources in place for marketing, will free you up to focus on your core business of practicing law with better preparation and in a confident manner. Also, this approach has the added advantage of helping you avoid many unanticipated problems as well as costs and expenses that can potentially wreak havoc with your practice. And because you have a plan in place you can make operational decisions more easily and make decisions more quickly and effectively.

Planning also benefits your firm's employees, keeps them on task relative to both their short-term goals and the bigger picture goals of your firm, makes them perform tasks more efficiently and overall typically increases their productivity. You will also have both quantitative and qualitative tools in place to evaluate employee performance, and, when necessary, work to develop employees in their areas of need—all actions which will result in your practice functioning at optimum levels. And just as you measure your own progress against your short-term objectives, you must check-in to speak with each employee to assess at what point he or she is relative to reaching his or her short-term goals. Many experts in and outside of law suggest these check-ins should occur weekly in the space of short 10 to 20 minute intervals.

Though more on communication with you staff will be discussed in Chapter 8, when checking in with employees be sure to encourage them to share their insights. Whether you agree with a suggestion a staff member makes, the employee will always come away from a discussion believing that he or she has a voice in the firm and that his or her opinion is respected and valued. Keep in mind, too, that because employees are in the trenches and immersed in the day-to-day activities of maintaining case files, answering calls and regularly dealing with clients, they may have a much closer, more accurate perception of what is and is not working.

Seeing is believing

A powerful and consistent emotion can be one of the strongest motivators and what pushes you to achieve in your career as well as in your practice. When talking emotion, however, we're talking right brain, that part of the brain where creativity, visualization, nonverbal feelings, imagination and intuition are found. Lawyers, judges and bankers tend to be left-brained, according to an article in *Psychology Today*. This stands to reason because the left side of our brains is where our logic, analysis, language typically the aptitudes of lawyers, make their home.

It may seem odd that lawyers would use emotion to launch their business plan. The truth is, however, that drawing on nonverbal feelings to mentally picture what we want to achieve begins to bring goals to life. Then taking action by cutting and pasting representative clippings from magazines onto poster paper to make a vision board makes them tangible. These are steps that many prominent and accomplished business people in all fields attribute to their success. We also know this first hand. We've created vision boards individually and collectively at our firm and can candidly say, it really does work.

Whether we describe ourselves as right brained or left brained, we are all, in fact, a balance or blend of the two. Still, while these two halves work differently, most of us are not 100 percent vested in one side. Therefore, despite the left-brain tendencies of most attorneys, addressing inspiration can be a powerful way of driving home the goals of a strategic plan. You can balance out the sterility of a written business plan by augmenting it with a small vision board, says Susan Solovic, in her blog The Small Business Expert. "By capturing images on a vision board for business purposes, you can make your ideas and inspirations come alive in a way that is impossible with a formal business plan," she says. And Solovic is not alone in her thinking. Oprah popularized the vision board concept and said her vision boards were a large factor in building her empire.

Solovic emphasizes that a vision board for a small business—or in this case, a law firm—can add a dimension to how the entire staff relates to practice leadership in ways that are "impossible if your only 'guide' is your original written business plan. "We all need inspiration from time to time and we should be honest with ourselves about that need. We all should be daring enough to try something that might be out of our comfort zone."

Chapter To-Do's and Takeaways

Always remember: Your business is a constant work in progress. You need to continually evaluate and edit to move the ball forward.

Short-term goals build incrementally toward the achievement of your long-term goals. Without them, your big picture plan will never be implemented.

Attainable, but with a stretch: this is the desired description of a short-term goal.

No team or practice can focus on more than two wildly important goals (WIGs) at the same time.

There's no shame in failure if you've given it your best shot. The key is to learn from failure and leverage your success.

Creating a vision board brings a sense of purpose to the goals you establish to develop yourself professionally and build a successful practice.

Here are some tools to get you up and running with your vision board.

Gather together a ton of magazines, a good supply of glue or a super large glue stick, markers, stickers and anything else that will help you portray your goals and dreams.

Select images of the things you want to achieve.

Include some visuals that represent the feelings that will be created from reaching your goals. For example, if you're an elder care attorney you might post a photo of an elderly person looking happy as she settles in to her downsized home; if you're a land use attorney, you might show a photo of eager consumers shopping at the new mall that's built on the tract of land on which you negotiated terms with the municipality in which the mall is located.

Make your own vision board or gather your colleagues together and make one that visually represents the goals of the firm.

Once you've created your vision board, place it in a special space in your office or cubicle. Having it constantly in your line of sight can inspire your own visualizations during short time outs in your work day. Research shows that mental exercise can influence what you achieve in life. For example a study looking at brain patterns in weightlifters found that the patterns activated when a weightlifter lifted hundreds of pounds were similarly activated when they only imagined lifting. In some cases, research has revealed that mental practices are almost effective as true physical practice, and that doing both is more effective than either alone.

CHAPTER 4

A Self-Driving Car Gives You the Ability to Have Deeper Conversations With Your Passengers

If you can't describe what you are doing as a process,
then you don't know what you are doing.

-W. Edwards Deming American
Engineer, Statistician, Professor,
Author & Lecturer

You probably use dozens of processes every day. You may go through the same steps every time you complete an intake form for a new client, solve a problem when a client calls in on the phone or reach out to someone new and provide more information about your firm.

It's great when each process moves along smoothly and your daily operations run like clockwork. But continually execute an inefficient process,
and the results can prove disastrous.

Processes are designed to streamline the way that you and your team work.

Processes that don't work can lead to problems…like

▶ Customer complaints about poor product work quality or
    bad service

▶ Colleague frustration

▶ Work duplication, or incompletion

▶ Cost increases

▶ Resource waste

▶ Bottlenecks and missed deadlines

That's why, when processes go awry, it's important to step back and figure
out what's wrong and chart a course correction.

When everyone follows a well-tested set of steps, there are fewer errors
and delays and less duplicated effort. What's more, because the well-tested
steps of a process sets expectations, clients come away from a call or meeting at your firm feeling satisfied and your staff leaves the office at the end
of a work day feeling accomplished knowing he or she has done a good
day's work.

Unfortunately, sometimes it seems easier to muddle through with poor
methods of doing things rather than facing up to a bad situation, taking a
timeout to review what isn't working and then reflecting and brainstorming a way to make a change. At some point, we've all been at that place

where forging on—even the wrong way—seems less time consuming than stepping back to review, reflect and change.

But when that trash talk of "don't take the time" rears its ugly head, beat it down. Because taking the time to rework your processes will streamline your operation and save you time in the long run. Plus, you'll also have the benefit of the improved efficiency that will make for a happier, less burdened staff, and clients who are more satisfied with your service. The efficiency of workflow processes must be a primary goal at your firm.

The power of SWOT analysis

Involving your staff, is a must for problem solving in your workplace. Typically, your firm comprises employees who perform various roles in the organization from office manager, to paralegal to clerical and administrative staff. No matter what process you're focused on, having this combined group of people put their heads together makes the difference between ho-hum or top drawer solutions.

Now that you have your team together, experts recommend that you have them conduct a SWOT analysis, an organized list of your business's greatest strengths, weaknesses, opportunities, and threats. SWOT is an analytical framework that can help your company face its greatest challenges and find its most promising new markets. The point of a SWOT analysis is to help you develop a strong business strategy by making sure you've considered all your firm's strengths, weaknesses, as well as the opportunities and threats it faces in the marketplace.

Strengths and weaknesses are things that you can change in your business such as location, employees, and marketing, client onboarding or callback procedures. Opportunities and threats are things outside of your business, things over which you have no control like competitors or changes in client or market needs.

The primary objective of a SWOT analysis is to help organizations develop a full awareness of all the factors involved in a decision, action or short- or long-term plan.

SWOT analysis can serve as a precursor to any sort of company action, such as exploring new initiatives, making decisions about new policies, identifying possible areas for change, or refining and redirecting efforts mid-plan. It's also a great way to improve business operations to make sure they're effective and addressing the right things, and efficient, doing things, presumably the right things, right.

Sometimes lawyers as well as the staff at a legal firm think about what's right at the firm and ways to improve what's wrong, but they never commit their ideas to writing. That kind of informal planning shortchanges any process improvement effort. Among other things ideas are never fully thought out and reviewed and challenged by other sources.

On the other hand, writing—and in this case—following the four structured SWOT categories at the start of your evaluation, assumes a commitment to both evaluation and execution. What's more, it democratizes the action, exploring ideas from all personnel, not just you or your partner who may be too immersed in the facts of a case to see beyond a blind spot. But because your staff is often your firm's first point of contact with clients, they may be able to offer up new perspectives to mitigate a procedure—perhaps even targeting some other issue unknown to you that may be the source of a problem.

A widely-accepted template for a SWOT analysis is four-squared table listing elements, strengths vs. weaknesses and opportunities vs. threats, though others recommend a simple listing of the strengths, weaknesses, opportunities and threats categories. Whatever format you choose will work as long as you take a thoughtful approach to filling out the analysis categories. You and all who participate must be truthful and tough, turning the components you are looking at inside-out to achieve a thorough and honest assessment.

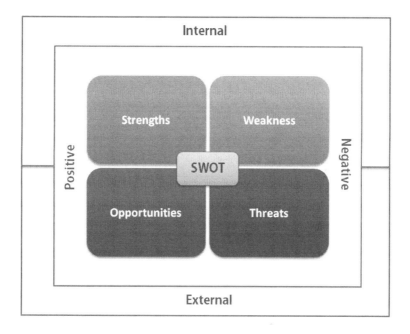

Courtesy Google Images

Keep in mind that strengths and weaknesses are internal. That could include anything from the culture you've created at your firm, to the expectations you set for yourself and your staff and the accountability you and your staff have relative to productivity and performance. It can also include the processes you've initiated—anything from onboarding new employees and the benefits and rewards (e.g., bonuses, raises, or praise) you give them, to the way you onboard and welcome new clients and adequately maintain their case histories and field their questions, to what software you're using to run your practice.

Though these top two elements, strengths and weaknesses, are not specif-ically correlated to the bottom two, opportunities and threats, they may indirectly relate. For example, a weakness could be exemplified by the fact that you and your partners do not attend enough networking events because you're chained to your desks after hours catching up on your cases. If this sounds like you, you may be thwarting market opportunities to expand your client base.

Acknowledging this as a weakness and correcting it may mean that you and/or your partner could make a concerted effort to meet more people, join more organizations related directly or tangentially to your firm's core focus and ultimately have more opportunities for referrals that would potentially expand your client base. It might also mean that you designate your top paralegal, who's knowledgeable, communicative and social, to represent your firm in an organization.

Beyond networking, these external factors represent issues that you or your firm do not directly control: shifts in client needs; new products and technology for law practices; financial, real estate or employment trends; demographics around your practice; political, economic or government regulations and compliance requirements; and relationships with other professionals directly or indirectly related to your core practice focus.

And now what?

Completion of your SWOT analysis does not mean you are by any means done. You must come up with recommendations and strategies based on your findings, and leverage your strengths and overcome your weaknesses, using your strengths to exploit opportunities and combating threats as best you can.

Many experts say this is the time and place where strategy development provides a firm with the best opportunity to be creative. It's a time when staff members can work together for the betterment of the firm and a time when innovative ideas and practices can emerge. What's more, the intrinsic value gained from being part of that process can do wonders for the morale and the culture of your firm. It can also go a long way to setting you on the right course with your processes. Consider how that will improve your ability to cover tasks when an employee is sick or on vacation—even better, how prescribed processes will improve the onboarding and training so vital to a company's success.

One last reminder: A SWOT analysis isn't a one-time event. Your firm, like any firm, continues to evolve as it grows. Therefore, you should engage in the SWOT analysis process periodically. Some businesses perform it yearly, others quarterly or biannually. Others engage in it when they are midstream in ushering in a new process to evaluate how well it's working, or as part of due diligence when they are considering adopting a new technology application, developing an area which could expand their core practice area or other such decision vital to the firm's operation and growth.

Taking the time to review your processes, identify what isn't working and then reflecting and brainstorming on improvement approaches will keep you and your employees from getting bogged down with the press of daily operations. It will also empower you to be successful at work **and,** because you are functioning more efficiently, you will also be more present and feel more fulfilled with family and friends in your personal life.

Chapter To-Do's and Takeaways

Regardless of how well your firm is performing, external changes— changes in compliance laws, a new competitor in the neighborhood, clients no longer in need of your services, or an onslaught of new ones—could pose threats to your firm's success. It's imperative that you recognize these threats and do what is necessary to meet them.

Avoid adopting an "if it's not broke don't fix it" mentality—perhaps one that is even ill-conceived. To ensure your firm's productivity and profitability, the rule of thumb is to <u>regularly</u> take the time to step back to evaluate your processes to make sure they are yielding the results you want and need for both your employees and your clients.

While we will delve into the below areas in upcoming chapters, here is a checklist that will help you identify some areas for review:

Employee guidelines and training

Do you have a manual that includes standard operating procedures for the firm—the guidelines, rules and regulations and set of expectations by which everyone in the firm top down and bottom up must abide? And, accompanying this, do you schedule training for all your new hires? If not, it's important to change that. Providing training to new hires enables them to understand the values and goals of your organization. What's more, training must be repeated at least annually for *all* employees to ensure that everyone is operating within the same set of overriding standards and parameters.

Employee communications

Do you communicate with your staff or are you too busy juggling all the elements of your cases to do so? Being visible and dialoguing with your employees is imperative—to show interest in what they're doing, to recognize their achievements, to find out if they have all the tools to produce at the level your firm requires, to have them tell you what's working as well as where there are gaps. You must also be "on the floor" with your employees daily or several times weekly.

Time management

How are you spending your work day—especially when you're not meeting with clients, at offsite meetings, at town hall or in court. Are you spending too much time on paperwork, other administrative tasks or fielding less complicated client calls, thus making you less effective as a partner and/or head of your firm? In fact, do you feel overwhelmed by paperwork to such an extent that you're spending too much time trying to find documents important to a specific case? Knowing how to delegate administrative tasks to staff admins or other administrative personnel will open-up more hours for you to focus on your high-level legal work and set the bar for your firm.

Marketing and networking

Word-of-mouth (WOM) marketing may be successful, and there's nothing better than a referral from a satisfied client. WOM, however, is not a one-sided activity. Your job is to be proactive in cultivating new relationships. Keep in touch with former clients or professional contacts by an occasional call or handwritten note to find out how they're doing, asking them to lunch, a one-to-one sit down over coffee, or a game of golf; or accepting that long-ago invitation to be a visitor at a professional organization to which they belong. This puts you in the position to learn more about them, discover possible alignments and/or to be a go giver who pays it forward. Solid relationships are at the base of growing law practices.

Client onboarding

Do you have a comprehensive questionnaire and information sheet to survey new prospects? An intake form will provide a wealth of information that will make you more knowledgeable during your first sit-down with an individual. It will also enable your support team to get enough of a sense of a prospect and his or her issue to know whether it's you or your partner who can best handle a case.

Phone calls

Are you spending too much time fielding inconsequential client calls? Better notetaking requirements on the part of everyone in the firm will keep all records up to date. This practice supplies subordinates with the information to make callbacks and handle some client questions. Clients receive responsive service and you can redirect your time to the legal aspects of a case.

CHAPTER 5

Get Your House in Order: Time-consuming but Necessary

For every minute spent in organizing, an hour is earned.

-Benjamin Franklin
President of the United States
of America (1785-1788)

Have you ever walked into the law offices of one of your peers to be greeted by bulging rust-colored files and piles of paperwork? We certainly have.

We don't know about you, but for us that look makes us feel a bit claustrophobic, but more importantly, unsettled and unsure. There is nothing that saps the confidence of your clients more than the look of disorganization in your office. It begs the question: Can this attorney actually handle my case?

Even if you're the best attorney on the planet, that fear may be a realistic concern for your client. Because there is nothing like disorganization to dispel client confidence in the competency of your firm—and frankly, to interfere with your ability to get the job done.

At this point, three key facts inform your future actions.

> **Number One**: Your clutter needs to be cleared.
>
> **Number Two**: You must turn to your staff to help with the cleanup.
>
> **Number Three**: Acknowledge that the organization that follows the tidying establishes an environment conducive to efficiency in workflow going forward.

Well-prepared tactical work guides, supports and refines your final product, productivity, says productivity expert Laura Stack in her *Doing the Right Things Right*. And, productivity enables the execution of your business plan, the attainment of your short-term goals and, ultimately, the delivery of you mission.

An additional benefit: Pinpointing a staff member to help with this chore gets you thinking about individuals you can trust—a paralegal who is familiar with the law and a clerical staff member who follows directions and has what human resources expert David P. Jones calls a can-do/will-do attitude in his *Million Dollar Hire: Build Your Bottom Line One Employee at a Time*. Plus, including them in this process exposes you to their organizational ideas and establishes a base for the way you will delegate work and manage procedures in the future.

But, first things first…

Let's get physical

Clearing the stacks and perhaps even thinning out the folders may take some time, but this will pay dividends in the long run. The initial task involves looking through the papers and categorizing them into stacks that will require a second action. The stacks will include:

- ✓ Pieces of ongoing files on which work has been completed and require filing in a client file (mostly, originals)

- ✓ Pieces that must be scanned and stored electronically. (mostly, everything other than originals

- ✓ Pieces that require photocopying (mostly, copies that need to be mailed out to clients)

- ✓ Pieces from cases now closed that require filing in closed files that now require archiving (again, scanning)

- ✓ Copious law newsletters, magazines and other letters that may be beneficial research reading at some point (organized library)

- ✓ And, finally, there will be junk mail and other items that likely don't require a stack but should go directly to the waste paper basket (the scariest yet best feeling)

Admittedly, there will be some supervision on your part. For starters, you can identify the stacking categories. Based on the above, we suggest the following:

- ☑ To work on now

- ☑ To work on later

- ☑ Delegate filing

☑ Delegate scan for anywhere/anytime access

☑ Delegate photocopying

☑ For research and reading

☑ For disposal

"To" is for you to do.

"Delegate" is for others to do.

"For" is for you to file for reference or dispose of immediately.

Out of sight, out of mind—but easily accessible. That's the theory.

Once the stacks are complete, you may have to review them to make sure everything is categorically in order.

But once everything is blessed and put away, and you can once again see your desk and credenza tops, you will feel like a new person!

But think a bit further. The staff members who helped you now know where everything is located which means they can put their fingers on something *quickly* as needed. And this lays the foundation for your next step: delegation. You are now ready to entrust others to some actions and tasks—something, if you have let things pile up, you likely have not been doing.

Remember our previous chapter's discussion of process improvement. Delegation, which we'll discuss in depth in chapter 10, is an important part of that. Here's your chance for a significant process improvement. Once you institute process improvement you will see a big change…and you will feel unburdened, lighter, more energetic and ready to take the next important step.

Chapter To-Do's and Takeaways

The organization of your workspace creates an environment conducive to productivity for you and your staff.

An organized physical space unclutters the mind and staves off the feeling of being overwhelmed.

An organized environment reinforces client confidence in the way you will manage their cases and provide solutions to their problems.

A successful firm is reliant on the participation of all staff members not just the firm's founders or partners. Easy access to all documents by appropriate staff facilitates participation and the speed and efficiency with which they manage their work. Workspace organization contributes to that.

By creating an environment of learning and trust you enable your staff to accept additional responsibilities with confidence, not timidity and fear.

CHAPTER 6

The Inbox Theory™: *Lean and Clean*

Back to Basics: Out of sight. Out of mind.

-Clelia Pergola

Ah email. Despite the pluses, it's a time sapper that can interrupt work-flow and hamper productivity. Time loss compounds the problem of never feeling caught up at work, and knowledge workers like lawyers, need huge chunks of time to complete work, says Tom DeMarco co-author with Timothy Lister of *Peopleware*. An interrupt includes the time of the inter-rupt plus an additional 20-to-25 minutes to get back into the groove-state psychologists call flow."

While there has been much written about ways to avoid email interrupt (e.g., turning off alerts, disciplining yourself to check email only once or twice a day) there has been little published about what the information overload of email looks like—how your inbox looks as it continues to grow. Just look at your overstuffed inbox. Pressure mounts as you contemplate your required replies. While ignoring the emails often seems like the easiest way out, it is likely that a huge knot develops in the pit of your stomach. The emotional implications of that can impede workflow, too.

Then, what's your alternative if your inbox is full?

Take charge of it with this two-step process:

The Inbox Theory™
Step 1: Create subfolders

- ✓ Active

    - ○ Add Sub-Folders such as Clients, General Office, Departments in your firm; Old Emails are a MUST

    - ○ Folders with Diverse Subjects and Tasks [e.g., news from organizations to which you belong, continuing education notices, changes in aspects of the law related to your practice area

Step 2: Earmark an Action

- ✓ Start Moving! Select ALL Emails and move all into Old Emails Folder

Now the theory is in sight and an action is required from YOU! If it is a list serve, informative email, it goes into a specific subfolder such as Legal Research. If it is related to a matter you should add the notes to the Clients' Notes file, we will discuss in Chapter 7, or forward to an assistant or paralegal who is responsible for filing it because it is an administrative duty.

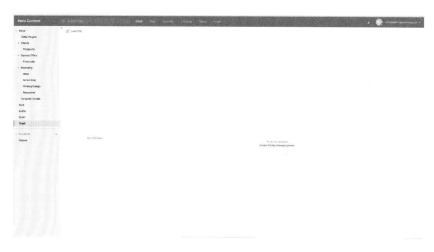

Courtesy Clelia Pergola

Much like the Out of Sight Out of Mind theory described in Chapter 5, the subfolders you have created can be shared with staff. Because they have access, they can get at what they need *quickly.* And once again, this creates the perfect opportunity for delegation and a time when you entrust others with some actions and tasks. It's another big step toward process improvement and a big change that will considerably help to lighten your load.

Because your inbox fills up quickly, you will have to determine how many times a day and at what intervals you will go through this process. Then, discipline yourself accordingly. The good news is that each time you'll be greeted by fewer emails, and you will have the calm and confidence of knowing you have taken charge. Always begin with deleting the spam emails, then proceed to the emails that you will "read later." Next, you want to read the informative emails from clients who do not require a response; you may forward these to an administrative staff member to add in the notes page.

At last you are left only with those items on which you need to work and respond.

The Outbox Theory™

If you really want to get organized, you can manage your outbox (sent folder) as well. Your outbox is generally less onerous than your inbox. Because you're the sender, you're in charge to some extent. Nonetheless, there's also power in keeping the number of sent emails at bay in your outbox and relegating them to appropriate folders following the moment you hit send. Plus, it makes them more easily searchable when you must go back and confirm or cross-reference a past action.

Again, a two-step process is required. [Suggest another screen shot here]

Follow the rules we demonstrated earlier and move the emails into their designated folders. The only ones that remain in your outbox are emails you sent to clients, prospects, strategic alliances etc. because you are waiting for a response to these. It is a way to manage your outgoing requests most of which typically fall by the wayside because you lose track of them.

With the Outbox Theory, only the emails for which you are awaiting a response are left in your outbox. This enables you to focus on responses, taking action quickly upon receipt of a response or following up with a second request to those emails that remain unanswered.

It's about how this feels

The Inbox and Outbox Theories enable you to manage email in an orderly manner. If you follow this system daily, you will feel the sense of calm that comes with being in control of this once very time-consuming and onerous part of your daily workload. Even better, you will feel more accomplished because you will be productive and more in charge of not only your email, but also your work and your time.

There's nothing like the impact of a very lean in- and- outbox. Enjoy!

Chapter To-Do's and Takeaways

Each day, focus on managing one day's emails.

Take a same day approach to those things that can be managed quickly: deal, delegate, destroy, defer.

Make your emails part of a to-do list on your daily planner.

Take your name off the subscription lists of organizations and newsletters that provide information that is no longer of value or relevant to you.

CHAPTER 7

It's All in the Notes

Quality is not an act. It is a habit.

-*Aristotle*
Greek Philosopher & Scientist

Communication is key to the attorney client relationship. While the outcome of a case may not result in achieving what the client wanted, your level of service, your effort and attitude define a client's satisfaction with the way you managed his or her case.

Timely and frequent communication with your clients to keep them abreast of case status at any given time or to answer any questions or address their uncertainties are the keys to client satisfaction. Your ability to perform in this area is reliant on your case notes.

It has been noted by those who consult on law practice efficiency that attorneys, in particular, and in many cases their staff, are overwhelmed by the sheer volume of data that surrounds their daily work—be it the print, paper and copious written file data or the many electronic documents and emails and status updates that are part of any case. Still, attorneys and their staff by nature are inclined and trained to accommodate the client needs related to billable hours. Even if a system isn't totally broken, firm members have typically learned to compensate through roundabout ways which likely take longer. Eventually they retrieve information, piece it together and respond as best they can to client demands and calls.

Lawyers, of course, write their to do lists on legal pads and during interviews or client phone calls scribble copious notes. Many people, including lawyers, love legal pads. But say what you will about them, one of the main things wrong with them, particularly for lawyers, is their capacity for scribble, and their randomness. Deciphering the scribble is hard enough. Beyond the chicken scratch, case for the same case are taken on different legal pads in the office, the conference room, the court, your car. They become difficult to sequence. Even worse, they go astray—a fate akin to there being no notes at all.

The efficiencies of the technological age have given us tools that make up for the shortcomings of the legal pad. That's good news. Good legal business practice requires often copious and certainly clear notes to track what you have done on a case, what's still pending and requires action, with whom we have spoken, what we talked about and when.

Beyond efficiency, such recordkeeping is also critical to maintaining compliance with ethics rules. Communicating with clients in a timely and effective manner is a requirement of the American Bar Association (ABA) Rules of Professional Responsibility. Failure to do so is not only a violation of these rules but an instance for disciplinary action.

The paperless option

One of the best ways to avoid violations is to go paperless. While not necessarily a prerequisite, dumping your legal pad to go paperless will go a long way to ramping up your firm's efficiency. Even if your practice does not convert to a paperless environment, it is strongly recommended that you create an electronic file for each client. Going paperless or having an electronic file in which you integrate some document management capabilities means you can rely on matter centricity through a document and email management system that allows you to organize and retrieve everything for a particular case or client—documents, email, case information, notes—all in one place.

The approach is best described by the term matter-centricity which was coined in 2002. The concept is based on housing information in multiple repositories that are either centralized through a document management system or linked together with a common identifier such as a client's unique "matter" billing number. This concept benefits attorneys as the ease of storing and finding client information becomes more efficient. With the proper storing of client information under a unique matter number, your firm now has more control over intellectual property. This means that anyone in your firm from an admin on up with permitted access to the case file can be quickly responsive to client needs and participate in keeping a client up to date.

While there are many document and record management systems available specifically geared to law firms and centralization, storage and functionality, a new technology solution isn't a one-step operation in which the technology is installed and your staff starts using it. It is also likely that as a smaller firm, you may try to update your legacy system. That is why you must establish a process and policy to determine how you will centralize client information, store it and retrieve it.

Get everyone involved

For most firms, centralizing data is a significant undertaking which requires employees top down and bottom up to change their way of doing things. Behavioral reorgs like this can be challenging, because by human nature it's hard to change the way we do things, even if the way we've been working isn't totally efficient.

This is compounded by the fact that attorneys and their staff by nature are inclined and trained to accommodate the client needs related to billable hours. Even if a system isn't totally broken, firm members have typically learned to compensate through roundabout ways which take longer but eventually help them retrieve information, piece it together and respond as best they can to client demands and calls.

To ensure buy-in to either new technology or better ways of doing things, you will benefit from forming a committee that includes every grade level of employee at your firm—or if your firm is small enough, everyone at the firm—and solicit their suggestions.

Process supports policy

A reliable process and template for collecting and storing client information is necessary to bring your policy to life. You and your team must also determine what content must be included in the case information so as to provide anyone who subsequently reads the file a thorough account of what work has been done to date and what actions are still pending.

What's more, processes must clearly define roles and responsibilities—in other words, who can "touch" a client file, and to what level of action. Keep in mind, that your firm, like all legal firms, faces ethics and risk management issues. Compliance in terms of proper client management is one of the largest. Your job, then, is to ensure your firm has a strategy in place to manage client material ***consistently*** so you are always at the ready to act when the need arises and at the same time act compliantly and appropriately.

Above all, new policies and procedures must be memorialized in writing and included in your policy manual. Plus, all staff, yourself included, must be trained on these new policies and procedures geared toward centralization. When new personnel come onboard, they must become educated on the policy and be trained in compliant usage.

Ready to take notes

Now that you have the technology policy, process and compliance tracking in place, you are ready to set up a robust notetaking system. Good detailed notes are the base of any document management system and are a boon for maintaining compliance involved with your firm's risk management challenges and, of course, your provision of good client service.

Here are the things your case notes should include:

- ✓ Client Name

- ✓ Client File (Matter) Number

- ✓ Name of Person Fielding Action

- ✓ Reason for Action

    - ° Client Initiated (e.g., email, letter or call)

    - ° Initiated by third party (relevant governing organization or court, etc.)

    - ° Directed by a member of the firm

- ✓ Description of Client Contact (if applicable)

✓ Resolution of Client Contact if Client Initiated

✓ Pending Actions

✓ Completion of Action if Internally Directed

✓ Deadlines Attached to Action Items Resulting from Client Discussions

✓ Callouts to Colleagues Needing Alerts on This Call

✓ To Do

An important note: While you should design a case notes template to which all members of your firm have access, make sure your Description of Client Contact section is set as an unlimited text field so that you can provide a ***full account*** of your meeting, phone call, etc.

Organize with tags: Depending on the sophistication of your technology, you may be able to set up a case note system that allows you to add tags, icons that hold special significance. For example, you may be able to add a tag that says "schedule" or "calendar" so that your admin can review a recent case note and continue the delivery of service by scheduling a necessary meeting between you and your client. "Email" may be another tag which will allow you or anyone who needs to review the file to look at recent emails that include information about a case; similarly, a "documents" tag will remind you or direct you to look at an important document involved in your case.

If your case notes work in tandem with or are part of a document management system, a further level of sophistication will allow you to electronically interface with other important pieces of matter attached to a file. However, if you are still using a legacy system, integrating an electronic case notes template to monitor case actions, will enable you to provide better client service at the same time you are safeguarding your risk management and compliance.

Play your part

It's one thing to herald the value of standardized, centralized case notes; another to follow through on your commitment to them.

Important considerations and practices regarding note-taking:

- ☑ Follow any client phone call, by spending at least five minutes memorializing typing or dictating the content of your conversation into your case notes.

- ☑ Smartphone technology allows you to record conversations. This fosters responsive client service by enabling you to have an anytime/anywhere conversation with your client. Then either you or your admin must transcribe the conversation into your case notes format or dictate a note into your phone that conforms to your case notes template.

- ☑ You can share your notes with the client via email to ensure there is agreement on the content of the call and the actions, if any, to follow. This is a benefit if you are particularly concerned about your relationship with a client.

- ☑ Whatever the system you use to maintain your notes, make certain your case notes are always included in your clients' folders, whether these folders are electronic or print or both.

☑ Bottom line: File notes away every time you or a staff member
works on a file—even if the action is a simple as your clerical staff
member calling a client to say that you will get back to him or her
in the morning! Again, depending on your firm's document management system, this information must be retrievable easily and
quickly at all times.

Chapter To-Do's and Takeaways

Create an electronic file for each of your clients.

Never underestimate the value of case notes for providing exceptional,
responsive client service and for your firm's legal and ethics risk management and compliance. In tracking all your actions related to a case, case
notes can safeguard you against erroneous client claims that you have not
taken a specific or required action.

Include your staff in the creation of your case notes template.

Make sure roles and levels of responsibility of staff are clearly defined. This
will ensure that even the most well-intentioned of employees does not complete legal work that he or she does not have the credentialing to perform.

Train new staff and existing staff regularly on the need to maintain this
system and how to do it, then monitor usage and compliance.

Monitor usage of case notes employee-wide to make sure everyone is
always following procedures and appropriately using the system.

Recognize the value of case notes in furthering your firm's marketing
endeavors. Material in case notes can provide good content for case studies
and call out your differentiating actions to reach a favorable client outcome

and tie in to client testimonials. Your firm's website should include case studies and testimonials in their site's content.

CHAPTER 8

Reporting: A 360 Degree View of Your Business

Success is not final; failure is not fatal: It is the courage to continue that counts.

-*Winston S. Churchill*
Prime Minister of the
United Kingdom

Your law firm collects reams of data all day every day. Admittedly all this data can be overwhelming, but there is incredible value in it. Knowing how to use it for analysis and determine what metrics you should be tracking and measuring are critical to remaining profitable as a solo and/or small firm.

There is some controversy surrounding what to track. The first inclination is to track financial data. True, it's important. But numbers alone do not tell the whole story.

The bottom line for tracking and reporting is collecting information that will enable you to assess your performance. If you don't track your day-to-day, week-to-week and case-by case performance, you won't know how well you're doing and what's working and what's not.

You must identify gap areas and mitigate them to make your firm more profitable. The window to those efficiencies or lack of them is held in the case management reporting database which facilitates information sharing among staff, enhances work process efficiencies and results in better client service.

Case management systems have been around since the 1980's. Still, some firms have tried them and become discouraged because they did not experience an immediate return on investment. Others, with an allegiance to the ways of doing business that they are used to have been reticent to embrace technology.

Automate tasks to create, track, store and review matter

But case management systems enable the automation of routine tasks and afford law firms the direct practice management benefits of reporting by easily creating, tracking, storing and reviewing all matter pertinent to a case:

- ✓ All case information

- ✓ Contacts and stakeholders

- ✓ Documents and mail

✓ Email

✓ Notes and phone calls

✓ Appointments, tasks and deadlines

✓ Time, billing and expenses

✓ Research and other related product work

As important, ethics requirements for the practice of law now requires firms to develop their technological competencies to improve client service and bill clients fairly.

Indeed, case management systems allow you to automate the routine tasks that comprise a case from intake to completion and payments. All staff responsible for task completion on various aspects of a case or matter have access to the database so that they can provide status updates on their role in the process. Reports involve several stages: intake, pre-filing, discovery, litigation, resolution and payment and the various steps involved in each stage and for each service area in your firm.

Quick, substantive access fosters client-centric focus

Quick access to case-related information allows reports to be created almost instantaneously which ramps up responsiveness and strengthens your firm's relationships with its clients. Staff who field calls from clients can provide a detailed and intelligent update of the most recent developments in the case. When you consider the importance a firm's client-centric focus is to its growth and profitability, you might say the success of your firm is in large part riding on the wealth of information in this database.

Monitor workflow instantly from a centralized database

At the same time, case management systems and the reports your firm generates from them enable you to quickly monitor the workflow of all cases from a centralized database. This increases efficiency by allowing timely reporting to prevent costly mistakes from tasks overlooked or deadlines missed. It also fosters ready communication and collaboration of staff and teams involved in a case. Overall, this gives you the opportunity to better manage your firm's work process and course correct to improve handling as necessary.

Insight to staff resource allocation

The documented requirements bring clarity to functional requirements and provide a checklist that enables employees to be more self-sufficient when completing their assigned tasks, avoid duplication and be more accountable. Plus, the system facilitates onboarding of new hires by providing a consistent framework for training new associates, paralegals and support staff.

The case management reports will also give your perspective on what areas or functions may need additional staff to shoulder the workload, thereby affecting your hiring decisions or the way you allocate your current staff resources.

Eye to the future

Finally, the reports you generate enable you to review your cases to evaluate the types of cases that are most profitable to your firm. This will help you direct your future marketing and business development efforts.

Today's well-informed and savvy clients expect and demand effective and efficient service. Ultimately, it's all about your clients. Anything that improves client service hits your bottom line and bolsters your reputation, enabling you to retain clients for continuous or repeat business and making you a magnet for desirable new clients.

Chapter To-Do's and Takeaways

Case management systems and the reports they generate enable you to integrate and manage client and matter information and more effectively run your business.

Reporting is a key way to identify inefficiencies in the way you are doing business, managing cases and taking on clients, and target areas that require process improvements.

All told, case management systems and the reports they generate ramp up efficiencies in multiple ways:

- ✓ Provide access to all matter-related information and communications in a central location from a single interface

- ✓ Pinpoint immediately which matters your staff members or external parties individuals (i.e., opposing counsel, judges, witnesses, etc.) have been involved in and the status of those matters

- ✓ Simplify oversight to avoid duplication

- ✓ Save time searching for documents and other information

- ✓ Capture more billable time because of overall increased efficiencies

- ✓ Automate the new matter intake process

- ✓ Alert attorneys and staff when a new file has been assigned

- ✓ Create customized workflows via templates for each practice area, automatically populating documents with key matter information

Case management reporting provides a 360-degree view of your firm's daily operations, allowing you to project and plan for the future.

Reporting enables timely and quality interactions with your clients throughout the case management process, cultivating the customer loyalty and trust that will build your reputation and grow your business.

PART III

Embracing Your Team

CHAPTER 9

Communicate Within

*Your ability to communicate with others will account
for fully 85 percent of your success in your life.*

-Brian Tracy
Author and
Motivational Speaker

Like all professions, the legal profession is facing increasing client demands. The Internet and mobility have increased our connections to information and each other and made consumers more savvy and demanding than ever before.

Competition to attract clients and keep them is at an all-time high. Therefore, it is not uncommon for attorneys to prioritize communications to prospects and clients, to showcase their academic and professional credentials and, in the best case scenario, demonstrate to prospects and clients that the firm understands their needs.

This is important. But communications between lawyers and their teams is equally important. In fact, many experts believe that communicating with staff members builds such positive workplace relationships and becomes the important first step to client-centric/prospect-centric outcomes.

Effective internal communications separate productive and profitable firms from those that experience less than stellar results. In fact, firms risk losing those very billable hours they seek and let clients down because of poorly shared knowledge and disconnectedness that leads to missed deadlines, gaps in necessary tasks and poor client response time—all follow-ups to internal communications that are poorly defined and utilized. By contrast, clear, consistent and frequent communications in many forms are a must for staff to be engaged, feel a collegiality with the partners and their peers, and work effectively and efficiently as a team united in a common cause.

Communicating regularly to your employees in a manner consistent with the vision, mission and values of your firm as we discussed in Chapter 2, reinforces firm goals and communicates the sense that "We're all in this together." Just like at a large corporation, law firms, even the smallest of them, need to develop a strategic approach to internal communications and establish the policy, process and tools around it.

Communicating regularly to your firm also helps you retain great talent. It also increases your ability to recruit them. There is no better way to attract top talent and great clients than when satisfied employees get the word out about the great place they work.

Go Social

Today, communications are geared toward creating a sense of community and dependent upon digital connections. To accomplish this, smart firms are developing strong internal networks to move away from communications that consistently contain the views of leadership and instead encourage a dialogue of feedback from employees. Those two-way conversations lead to higher levels of commitment and motivation from staff and their greater sense of pride in the firm. Millennials and the digital generation have grown up with Facebook, Twitter and LinkedIn and they have high expectations for communications in a go social way. This means that whatever your age and your depth of experience you need to be plugged in to enrich the experience that people have of working at your firm.

It's important to understand that internal communications is a marketing initiative. The information shared should help everyone understand the firm's vision, mission and values and give employees a purpose in which they can believe. Also, the dialogue among firm leaders and staff members is proof that their achievements are recognized and their voices heard. The sense of satisfaction that builds is reflected in the way employees comport themselves at the office or talk about the firm inside and outside of its walls.

Not all there is

Still, while social media is an asset to internal communications, it should not be the only way in which you communicate to your team. Face-to-face communications are still vital. You can't over communicate, says Laura Stack. Plus, people receive and interpret information in different ways which means you must take care in what you say, how you say it, and when and in what format you say it.

Lay out your expectations concisely and clearly. Communicate overall firm expectations in a policy manual, however short, and reinforce them regularly in your conversations either formally through meetings or informally with your team. Individual projects pertaining to cases may also require specific instructions which can be delivered one-on-one. When a project requires a team effort, it's advisable to call a meeting and detail the work to be done and the expectations surrounding project completion. Then summarize the directives of your meeting in an email.

It's also smart to circle back to ensure understanding. This recommendation from Stack is a good one, because it is often overlooked with the over-emphasis on lauding self-starters. Sometimes the obvious isn't so obvious. Communications styles and the way people interpret idioms and information can lead to a misunderstanding of directions. Check in periodically to ensure directions are understood, progress is underway and whether any additional tools or resources are needed.

Focus on relationships

While this doesn't mean you try to be best friends with all your employees, it does mean you connect with your people as human beings, say Karin Hurt and David Dye, employee engagement experts and co-authors of *Winning Well: A Manager's Guide to Getting Results Without Losing Your Soul*. Treat everyone with respect and dignity, not as a number, object or problem. Build trust with, and between, your staff.

This includes listening to their values, needs and insights. When people have ideas, listen to them—not just the rising stars but everyone. Knowing they are heard and that their opinions are valued helps employees build confidence. Everyone's input makes a difference in a company; otherwise, you should question why you've asked an employee or employees to be a part of it.

This also includes helping them be and stay accountable. Encouraging accountability doesn't mean tearing a team member down when he or she makes a mistake. People must feel comfortable enough to make a mistake and be accountable for it without experiencing blame, guilt or fear. Clear and supportive communication create this kind of positive environment. What's more, your ability to deliver constructive criticism, cautiously and with a kind and measured tone, will go a long way to further an employee's professional growth and development.

Informal communications often help to build these relationships. Stopping at a staff member's desk to chat briefly to see how a person is doing is a collegial gesture. Again, asking how your colleague is doing with a project or whether there are extra resources or tools he or she thinks would be helpful not only shows interest but presents an opportunity to pull together any lose ends. Without being overly probing, you can also ask questions about an employee's personal life. For example, you might ask "How are your wedding plans progressing?" or "How did your oldest daughter's team fare in last night's softball game?"

You do this with your clients. Why not with your employees? Put yourself in their shoes, and think about what matters to them. Doesn't it feel great when someone remembers your name or an achievement that was mentioned in a recent last conversation? Lend an ear when they speak about their lives. Show interest.

Gratitude not guilt

And when it comes to relationship building, gratitude matters. It's always important to offer a thank you and a compliment when an employee has submitted good work, made an interesting suggestion or behaved in some small way that furthered the objectives or goodwill of the team. Make sure your words include a description of why and how an action made a difference. This is a helpful employee reminder about the way they interact with colleagues: You don't remember necessarily when someone says thank you but you sure do remember when they don't; always try to lead by doing the right thing and being respectable.

But relationships can also be broken and collegiality and trust destroyed if you lose control of your emotions. If you tend to react with emotion or anger when things don't go as planned, do whatever it takes to help get your emotions in check before speaking to an individual or addressing a problem.

What's more, relationships can be built or broken through emails or texts in which you lose the nuance of body language and tone. Be mindful of how you frame your words—and how you punctuate them. For example, when you use multiple exclamation points, question marks, capitalization or a combination of both, you are inflicting guilt. Behavior like this can offend and disturb the colleague or fellow managing partner who receives your message.

Effective communication starts from the moment new attorneys onboard at your firm. They are given case files and sent to their offices. Sit down and go over expectations—theirs as well as yours. There must be clarity about where you as members of the firm are heading; without this, they may head off to PF Changs and you to the local McDonalds. When employees fail at their jobs, you share the blame for not setting expectations.

Have fun

It's important to be serious about your work, but lightheartedness at work can lighten the load of a grueling day or that high pressure case. There's nothing like humor and laughter to inject some cheer into your workplace.

Also make it clear that you get that life happens. Everyone has bad days. Create a comfortable environment in which employees know that's okay.

Plus, choose words and actions that help an employee reset his/her bad mood.

And sometimes it's just about having fun. Create special occasions at which the team hangs out together, either by creating a fun activity during the work day or after work. At our firm, we schedule a regular Thursday team lunch at which we talk about where everyone is personally, professionally and health wise. Anyone who has a problem is free to discuss it with the team along with changes, updates or concerns about clients or the office. We also have weekly meetings at which we just all sit down and eat lunch together. It's like a family dinner; we all have our personal chairs and relax and feel free to just be ourselves. A friend who works in a small practice in New York says the managing partners take the team monthly after hours to Bowlmor where they bowl and play arcade games. And, a former colleague realized her support staff was spent from working on a complicated health care case. At 2 o'clock, she told everyone to stop, and then marched them all to the escalator and down to the movie theater and treated them all to a three o'clock show.

A strong internal communications strategy and the behavior to back it engage your employees, increase their productivity and encourage them to form a cohesive internal firm fan base. Internal fans create a buzz and energy that helps to get you noticed in the marketplace—that gets people to knock on your door when they encounter a legal matter that needs solving and keep you top of mind for when they do.

Chapter To-Do's and Takeaways
Consistent effective internal communications are an objective on par with the value of communications with clients.

Strong internal communications benefit client relationships and contribute to an increase in billable hours. The knowledge sharing and collaboration that result lead to thorough case management and responsiveness to clients.

Communicate internally to everyone. The receptionist who greets visitors or sorts the mail plays as important a role as you do as your firm's founder and managing partner.

Ask for opinions from staff members. This shows your respect for listening to their ideas and taking them into account. You may apply all or part of what they said, or make note of the idea as a workable option for the future.

When it comes to the Social Media side of communicating, be frequent and consistent.

And just as with external advertising, frequency, tone and consistency are important—often more than length and detail.

Welcome feedback—whether online or in-person.

Use employee communications to recognize and congratulate employees. This is an outstanding way to show you value their contributions.

Plus, the ability to communicate kindly with constructive criticism helps employees be/stay accountable and fosters their professional growth and development.

CHAPTER 10

Spread the Wealth: Delegate

In business things are never done by one person.
They're done by a team of people.

-*Steve Jobs*
Co-Founder, Chairman & CEO
of Apple, Inc.

Delegation, the art and science of entrusting a task or responsibility to another person, typically one less senior than yourself, is a critical best practice in business and law. And, yet, it is all too frequently misunderstood and underutilized and is the most underdeveloped management skill among leaders in all fields.

It is likely you have heard your colleagues complain they're buried in work, short on hours or days in the week as they try futilely to attend to their cases. Perhaps you have even commiserated.

The practice of delegation can wipe out the stress of being totally overwhelmed. In fact, when carried out properly, delegation provides incredible benefits to a firm—structurally, organizationally, culturally and monetarily—and this becomes more apparent as you break down the various touchpoints at which delegation will benefit your firm.

- ✓ **Plan and process** – You will have a plan and process in place that identifies the functional responsibilities of everyone in your firm.

- ✓ **Effectiveness and efficiency** – You will have identified the right tasks to complete project work and all of you will function more efficiently; you will do the right things right because the lines of functional responsibility will be clearly established. And because of this functional task list, everyone will be accountable for performance.

- ✓ **More clients. Better service** – When your firm is operating smoothly, you will take less time to complete work. And because you are operating at your peak performance level, you will inevitably provide better service.

- ✓ **Ramped up bottom line** – Put simply, because of the increase in volume of clients, you will pull in more revenue. As importantly, because of your enhanced service, you can charge more for your services.

If it's hard to argue these benefits, why is delegation so avoided? And why is getting it right so difficult? Answering these questions is a good first step in recognizing what may be holding you back from delegating or helping you identify how you may think you're delegating when in fact your execution is faulty.

The naysayers

People typically don't delegate because:

- ✓ They believe it takes too much time to show someone how to do something. Therefore, they end up completing task themselves, even if the task is beneath their pay grade—something that could be done by someone with less knowledge-specific education and credentials. That undercuts billable hours and is easily termed a time waster.

- ✓ They've delegated before, been displeased with the work and ended up redoing the work themselves.

- ✓ They treat it as an expense—perhaps a costly one—that will require them to increase their headcount, purchase new state-of-the-art apps, or require training to bring staff members up to speed on certain functions

- ✓ They feel insecure about giving up a piece of their case work or case load, fearing that the person who does the work will show them up

- ✓ They think they can do some of the more challenging parts of the work better themselves.

You will not be alone if any of the above mindsets hit home. In fact, in some ways, these beliefs are a manifestation of human nature. But , now, it's time to accept these tendencies as thought patterns and behaviors that need to be corrected to improve the way you work to better your practice, make it and your work days more efficient and, ultimately, live a better life.

Here are some strategies to get you in delegation mode:

Carve out the time beforehand

Deciding what to delegate is not an off-the-cuff occurrence. You will literally have to sit down, either with your partners, your staff or both, to think
through ways to streamline case work through shared functional responsibility. It may even take several meetings plus some independent time spent
soul-searching to accomplish this.

If you currently fall into the school of thought that delegation takes time,
you are right. But it's time well spent. The time you spend **prior** to putting
a system in place will pay dividends in spades in time saved and money
earned **down the road**.

Granted, if you're not used to delegating, this may be very difficult for you
at first. You may even panic at the thought that nothing you're currently
doing can be delegated. Admittedly, especially at first, targeting tasks for
delegation may take some self-discipline. Start by dissecting some of the
things you do into their skill requirements. Then focus on the tasks that
require the fewest skills, and determine how you will pass them off to
someone else, and recognize that you may have to teach or train your staff
members on how to complete the assigned tasks.

Part of the plan that you put together includes having a pretty solid idea
of whom among your current staff has the skill set or will-do attitude to
assume responsibility for a given task or function.

One good thing: Chances are, that tasks that fall under the same practice
areas are similar on all cases, enabling you to develop a plan that normal-
izes tasks for delegation.

Literally, you must chart out all aspects of the plan. Both the list of tasks to be delegated and the names of the people to whom they will be delegated. These must be memorialized in writing in two documents, that will be distributed to everyone in your office. And, remember, though cases vary, similar practice areas will require similar steps, so a global document can normalize the segments that can be farmed out.

One document will establish the policy and procedural guidelines for workflow that includes delegation; the other will be in spreadsheet, dashboard form that enables staff members to check in/check out of their start and complete task functions and also see the overall progress of a case or project as a whole. We suggest the guidelines be produced both in hard copy and live on your firm's Internet server. The dashboard must reside on a shared database to which you and the appropriate staff members have permissions for access.

Putting the plan into writing and spelling out the details clearly, makes everyone accountable—and this means you as well as your staff member. You must be accountable for providing necessary information, appropriate tools and reasonable completion timeframes, giving your colleague clear and proper direction for execution; your staff member must be accountable for status reports, if the task has a long tail, and for delivery. You and the person to whom you are delegating your task should agree on a deadline by which each assignment must be completed even if the action is not time sensitive. This helps to avoid procrastination and delays, and again makes stakeholders, including you, accountable for completion of the work.

Purchase tools and training

If delegation presents a whole new way of doing business at your firm, you may be on the hook to add some tools to the mix—and even some training. Perhaps a new document management system will facilitate delegation and the shared dashboard view related to project progress. If this is the case, training may be required to ensure that everyone in the office is trained on the correct usage of the system.

A different type of training might involve bringing in a consultant to speak on business process management in a law firm. This would not be a cheer-leading session, but rather a way to teach process management so that employees begin to experience during the training how the segmentation of functions into assigned tasks shared by staff members leads to a more efficient, less stressful and timely outcome.

Again, if you are currently of the school of thought that to delegate means to spend money, you may be correct. You need to recognize, however, that like with the allocation of time to develop the process, the spend for these steps *prior* to initiating these new systems will pay dividends on the back end.

You also must realize that training at regular intervals helps to keep your employees ahead of the curve on innovations in your industry, new com-pliance issues and improved procedures to name a few issues. This is a plus for your firm and its operating efficiencies. It also contributes to your employees' professional development generates goodwill and demonstrates that you are invested in them and willing to help them grow and develop in their careers.

Don't micromanage

You've spelled out the delegation details in writing, and instructed or trained your employees about the use of tools and the process. You're ready to launch, but your work isn't done. You must be continuously present for your employees in the process and continually drop by employee work sta-tions to see how things are progressing.

In carrying out this responsibility, it's important to understand the distinction between the casual, yet meaningful touch base versus micromanaging or nitpicking. Even with the best of intentions, we can all be subject to tunnel vision and fall prey to micromanaging. Micromanaging is characterized by pointed oversight and a very direct "how much have you accomplished," and potentially a tone of disapproval if things aren't going exactly as you planned or expected. That's not only off putting, but also nerve-wracking for the person on the receiving end—the person who wants to perform and do a good job. Plus, everyone has his/her own workstyle, and that individuality must be respected, too.

A genial conversation

This exchange, by contrast, is more of a conversation, and spoken like all conversations in a genial tone. And it's a conversation in which you are looking for feedback as much as you are getting a sense of where a person is with the work. It's more of "how are things going," and a "do you have all the information and tools you need to get the work done?"

You may even ask if he or she has suggestions about ways to improve the process to complete the work more efficiently. Discovering that there may be a better way to complete a task is a learning opportunity for you. It is also opens the door for your coworker to take the lead. And these are perfect times to praise your coworker for a job well-done or the sharing of a great idea.

At the end of the day, while these interactions may provide the opportunity for you to learn something, they most assuredly create spontaneous occasions to build bridges with your colleagues and staff. At a time when corporate loyalty is at a premium, authentically building bridges with your coworkers goes a long way to furthering retention—and retention is as much of a win for employees who want to advance in their careers as it is for the firm.

Surround yourself with the right people

When your goal is to create meaningful work teams and to staff them with people whose work is of a high caliber, you should always strive to hire the individual who is the best fit for the position and, overall, for your firm. To accomplish this when hiring, it's wise to consider not only an individual's experience and track record, but also evaluate his/her aptitude to learn new tasks and attitude to move out of the comfort zone to take on new challenges. Is this someone who right from the get-go—during the interview, actually—exudes excitement about your firm?

Hire for a combination of these traits and you'll hire someone who values your firm and the people in it as much as he or she values his or her own professional development and career advancement—someone who plays for the team and the betterment of the firm, not someone who's just working to bring home a paycheck.

A person who's always at the ready to learn and take on new tasks is a real asset, especially in an environment in which you delegate responsibility to others to complete pieces of the overall casework. Plus, if this individual is comfortable offering up suggestions, coming up with new and better ways of improving functions and processes and sharing ideas up to and including offering up constructive criticism, you will be working with someone who is at the ready to take on increased responsibility in your firm—someone who may want to move up from an administrative position to paralegal to get more involved with the law. And, if that becomes the case, offering that individual some form of tuition reimbursement will also result in an outcome that betters that individual as well as your firm.

Hiring the right people, means that as you delegate tasks, you will have to worry less and trust more that things will be done right.

Appoint a right-hand gal or guy

Over time, you may discover that you need some help in delegating tasks. You may decide to appoint a reliable coworker to divvy up the task responsibilities, teach, when necessary, how to attack the work, and oversee progress. This will surely free up more time for you to complete the legal tasks that align with your firm's billable hours. Even so, you must still allot some time to walking around the office to talk to your coworkers to check on their comfort level with the work, with your timelines for completion and for soliciting the feedback on how well the methods you and your right-hand gal or guy have created are working.

Change your perspective

By delegating, will you spend less time at the office or worrying about getting your case work completed? There's a good chance you will, but you'll definitely spend your office time more productively. Your hours at the office will be more directed to the practice of law and on execution more exclusively involved with high-ticket billable work—the skills you paid so dearly to learn in law school. Overall, the time you spend will matter more in completing the legal work your clients have hired you to complete. Plus, with other tasks farmed out, your cases will be handled in a more streamlined manner which means as a firm you will service your client in far less time.

What's more during your downtime on weekends, you will worry less about what isn't getting done, leave the office on Friday with a feeling of completion and be able to concentrate freely on doing the things you like to do in your free time along with spending time with friends and family.

Finally, by delegating, you will switch your focus from a task-oriented role—e.g., completing *everything* necessary to get casework completed—to a growth focus. Delegation requires you to take ownership of your leadership role and to switch your perspective on task management to fostering your firm's solvency and growth.

Chapter To-Do's and Takeaways

The time you spend *prior* to putting a system in place will pay dividends in spades in time saved and revenue the firm brings in *down the road*.

Hiring the right people means looking comprehensively at job candidates to evaluate not only their experience but also their aptitude and attitude for bettering the firm.

Hiring the right people, means that as you delegate tasks, you will have to worry less and trust more that things will be done right.

Done right, delegation provides the opportunity to build bridges and develop positive relationships with your coworkers.

Delegation requires you to switch your perspective on how you use your time. A commitment to delegate moves you away from a task-oriented focus to a focus on growth. Delegating allows you to take ownership of your leadership role in the stewardship and growth of the firm.

CHAPTER 11

A Little Bit Like Google

Ability is what you are capable of doing. Motivation determines what you do. Attitude determines how well you do it.

-Louis "Lou" Holtz
American Football Coach

The Google campus in Mountainview, Calif., represents the good life for employees.

Its much-publicized unconventional workplace design, huge and plentiful perks and the amazing freedom it offers to employees have become the subject of much conversation and the reason Google has been voted one of the best places to work by *Fortune* and the Great Places to Work Institute for many consecutive years.

Meeting rooms modeled after diner cars in lieu of conference rooms, tread-mill desk options because research has shown that walking while you work can be good for your health, 1000 campus bikes and a garden space to grow vegetables, free food that includes three meals a day and unlimited snacks, 20 percent of employee time allocated to doing what he or she wants, nap areas to snooze during the day….and the list of the rich perks Google offers its employees goes on.

Not every company can offer benefits to employees on the same scale. Still, at the core, the basic idea is pleasantly simple. Cofounders Larry Page and Sergey Brin understood people were successful in their jobs and loyal to their employers when they felt truly valued and thoroughly supported. Modeling that basic philosophy and borrowing some ideas from Google on even a small scale can create a culture of positivity, collaboration and creativity. All organizations should carefully consider what they can do to give employees the spaces and tools that enhance and support their work-day tasks as well as reinforce corporate goals.

Office design space to make the ordinary extraordinary

Architects focused on workplace design are adamant about design space in the knowledge economy. Their mantra: Focus on your office space if you want to build a high performance culture. This is an important concept for law firms, many which have been holding tight to the concept of the private office as a place in which lawyers can perform high value legal work with focus behind closed doors. But law, like many industries, is changing thanks to a host of factors: economic realities (e.g., the high cost of office space), technological advancements, new trends in the way people work, pressure from clients grown savvy by the incredible amount of information available to them. In short, ideal office design can create the foundation for a productive workplace.

Since 2008, Gensler, an international design and architectural firm, has done considerable research on work performance success factors and uncovered the importance of four work modes as the key work activities in the knowledge economy: focus, collaborate, learn and socialize. Gensler's proprietary Work Performance Index ^{SM} measures the time employees spend in each mode as well as a breakdown of the spaces used and how effective those spaces are for supporting each activity. While a workplace must be functional, it must also support human needs. Because employee engagement and satisfaction are key business drivers, Gensler's Workplace Performance Index survey uncovers opportunities to better connect the workplace with drivers of organizational effectiveness.

While Gensler's findings demonstrate that the attorney's office is not going away, they do show it is evolving. Its usage has been modified and minimized as has the surrounding space outside the attorney's office. In lieu of the stately mahogany desk which characterized the staid look of white shoe firms of yesteryear, today's attorney's office holds reconfigurable furniture which enhances functionality, is prime for interactive meetings with employees and integrates technology that accommodates in-person as well as virtual collaboration—all leading to improved workflow that's dependent on collaborative processes, not just individual work.

What's more, the confines of the individual office no longer define the workspace. Purposely created collaborative space provides open area areas in which employees may work, discuss shared projects and/or take a short timeout to chat with colleagues…attorneys included. In fact, according to Gensler's U.S. Workplace Survey 2016, the most progressive law firms have dramatically reshaped their workplaces. The most innovative of them are taking less space and collaborating more.

That said, lawyers still take full advantage of the fact that the private office is the most effective work space for all work modes. But, overuse of the office can work against an attorney and his or her firm. In fact, according to Gensler, the most innovative lawyers spend less time in their offices and more time in collaborative and communal space when compared to average-performing lawyers. "Pioneering firms are experimenting with furniture, ergonomics, technology and transparency to create more compact offices that fully support lawyers' need to think without distraction while remaining open and inviting," a Gensler spokesperson said.

Therefore, there is an opportunity for law firms to increase performance and reduce real estate and the cost associated with increased square footage by prioritizing shared space without sacrificing the benefits of the individual office.

Beyond your office

According to the survey, the most innovative lawyers leave their offices more frequently to work in various spaces within their office environments. These include conference rooms and open areas in which there are whiteboards and ample AV equipment to have several staff members participate in case discussions or calls with clients to which they are privy. When you adopt these practices as managing partner, you will have the chance to have face-to-face time with your staff and encourage more participation in case work as opposed to purely administrative functions.

While your conference room is a space to huddle over projects, it can and should double as a place for fun and offline conversations. At our firm, the entire staff convenes in our conference room every day to enjoy lunch. We also hold team meetings once a month as well as have team building sessions during which we talk about things that are important to us regarding work practices, firm policies and whether the way we are managing workflow helps to create the balance between our office and our homes. As an extension of these team building days, we collectively participate in fun activities; a popular one is getting together to create vision boards.

Just as Gensler has reported, learning is one of four key work modes. When it comes to work, learning is life long, office policies are evolutionary and individuals and teams must grow continuously. You can found your firm on principals grounded in collaboration and the space design and practices it nurtures and still regularly tweak your environment to make it more productive, efficient and fun. By soliciting employee feedback both in one-to-ones and via online surveys, you will identify tweaks to improve your processes. At the same time, you will see firsthand how the way you ask for employee feedback reinforces their engagement level and their understanding that they are contributing to your firm.

Meaning to their work

Seeing their recommendations come to life is rewarding and does much to build their confidence, feel comfortable with the risk of taking on higher level tasks and sharing their ideas—all which enhance their professional development. At the same time, this increases their loyalty and promotes retention, a win for you and the stability of your firm.

Involving staff in discussion of an interesting or challenging case is another way to make them feel appreciated and aware that you are supporting their professional development.

Even simple acts of kindness make a difference right from an employee's first day on the job. A warm welcome like "Hi. Nice to meet you. We're going to be working together," does much to cultivate a positive employee-employer relationship early on. In fact, Google data shows that when a manager welcomes a new employee on his or her first day, the employee end up 15 percent more productive in nine months, according to Lazlo Bock, who heads Google's People Operations Department.

Other rewards become perks employees also value: shortened Friday hours during the summer, a day off for a client case win in which they participated, a dinner for an employee and his or her spouse or significant other out as reward for completing work pre-deadline and even under budget.

As important, these rewards should be publicized in various ways. As an announcement within the office, on your firm's Intranet site, in a memo and on your firm's Facebook page. According to *Dr. Haiyan Zhang, IBM Smarter Workforce Institute*, the more channels used for recognition, the higher the employee's engagement level. This not only provides recognition to the employee but also puts them in a position to inspire and serve as a role model to their colleagues.

Goldberg Law has a Huddle Board. Team member names span the top of the board and all the goals run down the left side and include such actions as: helped a team member, made someone's day, handled a difficult situation well, completed a project. Every time a team member completes one of those tasks they get a tree, the Goldberg logo.

One important rule: You can only earn a tree when a team member acknowledges you completed that task and, therefore, gives you a tree. At the end of the month, prizes are distributed. These include gift cards for gas, spa visits, teeth whitening treatments at the dentist, an additional paid day off, etc. The rewards and recognition give something for staff members to strive for, and positive behaviors are developed not in an instructional way, but rather in the spirit of fun.

Goldberg Law Group Huddle

Goldberg Law Group, LLC
Elder Law | Estate Planning | Medicaid Planning

	Tonisha	Jessica	Marlena	Christina	Natalie					
Went above & beyond				✦						
Attention to detail		✦	✦							
Reached a goal										
Helped a team member	✦			✦						
Positivity			✦							
Proactive	✦									
Creative suggestion					✦					
Learned something new										
Completed a project		✦		✦						
Teamwork										

Gratitude matters

Sincere gestures of gratitude like those described above and other soft skills matter in the workplace, and law offices are no different. In a recent survey, Google employees weighed in on what makes a highly effective manager. As a surprise to even Google's higher ups, who as we noted earlier, are all about supportive work environments, employees rated traits like coaching, connection and empowerment. Technical expertise weighed in last. And, micromanaging was a real no-no.

Even-keeled was the top characteristic employees said they valued in their bosses. Employees said they appreciate managers who are patient, poised and positive. The Google employee wish list makes sense in law firms; when the workload is heavy and work and deadlines are high pressure, bosses who are impatient, too intense, unappreciative and tend to fly off the handle, only intensify the stress.

We also know of cases in which a managing partner rewards the four women on his staff by treating them to a weekend away to enjoy exercise, stress reduction classes and time at the spa.

Collaboration, coaching and an interest in employee lives

Managers who collaborate with employees by delegating to them, involving them in decision-making on certain issues and guiding them through challenging issues by helping them solve a problem instead of showing them what to do also topped the list. Again, your firm and your employees win: he or she learns traits important to his or her development and work is consistently completed with your standards.

While coaching and mentoring cultivate loyalty and trust among staff, employees in the Google survey said they also value managers who took an interest in their lives as well as their careers.

Compassion a workplace imperative

In their new book, *Awakening Compassion at Work*, Dr. Monica Worline, a research scientist at Stanford and CEO of EnlivenWork, and Dr. Jane E. Dutton, propose that it's either foolish or wishful thinking to imagine that suffering—a concept fundamental to human existence—could be separate from the immense investment of time and energy most of us spend at work.

Employees disengage or simply bide time at work when they feel their efforts are being overlooked. They are also upset when their bosses don't seem to care about their personal struggles such as a death in the family, divorce, family illness or their own health problems. Their personal emotional issues carry over into the workplace and detract from their performance. And when their employers don't acknowledge their suffering—when they seem uncaring—their unhappiness increases, causing more stress and a negative impact to their health.

Woline and Dutton reference the work of Compassion Lab Founder Dr. Peter J. Frost, who wrote in his "Why Compassion Counts" in *The Journal of Management Inquiry* that "suffering at work is a hidden cost to human capability." While acknowledging and easing suffering is not something most businesses, law firms included, consider when preparing a list of their firm's initiatives. Worline and Dutton say it should be.

Recognizing this costly oversight, managers and leaders who care deeply about the capacity of their organizations to operate with full human effectiveness will pay more attention to awakening compassion at work, these authors say. Compassion enhances collective capacities like innovation, service quality, collaboration, and adaptability.

It also leads to good health. Plus, walking the talk of good health provides another benefit. We suggest Lunch 'n' Learns about nutrition, stress and exercise. These other valuable health messages are another way for you to show employees you care about their well-being. Providing nutritious snacks as your budget allows is a thoughtful and beneficial frill as is the availability of filtered water.

Overall, modeling behaviors for good health like nutrition, hydration, exercise and leaving the office at an hour that allows rest and replenishment provide valuable paradigms for good physical and mental health. This practice also shows your staff they matter to you as individuals, not just as employees.

Chapter To-Do's and Takeaways

Google mandates a work environment that supports and values employees and bases it policies and practices on achieving this goal—including the way in which it designs its workplaces. Google's creation of a supportive work environment serves as a paradigm for other work environments.

No matter how small your firm, initiatives can be taken to create a Google-like atmosphere that nurtures employee fulfillment and engenders their loyalty and trust.

The design of your office has a tremendous impact on the way you relate to your employees and factors significantly into their comfort level and engagement and the meaning they derive from their day-to-day work.

Purposely created open office spaces foster collaboration, providing opportunities to coach and mentor your employees, solicit their feedback and recommendations and recognize them for the contributions and value they add to your firm.

Authentically giving recognition and rewards plays an important role in building relationships with your staff. They win by feeling respected and valued; you win by cultivating their loyalty and trust, which are prerequisites for retention.

Being accessible to your employees and showing you care about their personal and professional lives enhances their satisfaction and happiness at work and contributes to your culture, making your firm a place at which employees want to work.

Modeling healthy behaviors and providing some health-related perks demonstrate to your employees that they matter as people not simply employees.

PART IV

Put a Bow on It

CHAPTER 12: MARKETING AND NETWORKING

And Now Grow the Business

When you need a friend, it's too late to make one.

-Mark Twain
American Writer & Publisher

Now that you have an idea of what tools, tacks and strategies you need to run your practice efficiently, how are you going to get clients, old and new, to come through the door.

The answer obviously involves marketing and networking, which is an important part of marketing. It has been said that lawyers hate sales...or in terms more relevant to the practice of law, for the most part, lawyers hate developing new business even though most lawyers are by nature or education skillful communicators who it seems should do well at attracting new clients.

There's a natural tendency to shy away from things you don't like. Plus, with so much work on your plate and too little time, you may decide that marketing is best left to the professionals—an option that comes with a hefty price tag more suited to giant corporations.

The good news is that there are initiatives you can undertake on your own. They just take self-talk to get motivated and planning to lay out the structure of what you must do, when you must do it, and being accountable for doing it.

Networking, with its goal to build relationships, is one of the most cost-effective ways for solo and small firms to market and bring in new business. Networking leads to word-of-mouth referral business. The problem is, most lawyers don't know how or where to begin.

Start with your target market

The first important step is targeting the right audience. It has been said that attorneys often struggle with developing a concise, detailed description of their target market, but it is vital that you do this. By failing to do so, any marketing efforts you make will be hit or miss and likely futile.

When defining your target market, a good place to start is with your current client base. Getting a clear understanding of your existing clients is important because that demographic creates an ideal base for prospecting. Searching for the commonalities in their psychographics (e.g., their attitudes and aspirations and other psychological criteria) is helpful in creating a client persona.

Broadly speaking, people who have legal issues turn to attorneys. But get more specific. Within your practice area, drill down to some of the particular problems you solve and determine who and why someone would be willing and able to pay for your solutions.

Again, look at your existing and former clients and the revenue you pulled in from handling their cases. What specific problems and kinds of cases earned you the most revenue. From a bottom line perspective, those are the first level of clients you should be seeking.

But, where are those clients? As a small firm, you are likely pulling in clients from a circumscribed geographic area: the town in which you practice, surrounding towns or your county. That said, if you've developed a good rapport with your clients and network peers, you may be able to informally or formally poll them. You may be surprised to find that because of the level of service you provide to your clients, your reputation may proceed you. You may even be overlooking the potential for a larger geographic reach.

By asking questions of your client and peer group you might also glean some interesting information. For example, if you're a real estate attorney, a financial professional you know might make you aware that the global investment firm she works for will be opening a regional office in the next town. There's a good chance there will be an influx in population, an increase in the purchase of house and a potential for new business.

Another idea for expanding your target market would include specializing or creating a niche within your practice. While this could depend on your practice area, you could focus on a certain demographic. For example, we read of an estate planning attorney who created a very lucrative sub-specialty in asset protection for doctors and lawyers.

It's also always smart to be on top of what your competitors are doing. With a clear understanding of your demographics and psychographics, you can develop strategies to make yourself stand out from your competitors.

Once you are clear on whom you are going to serve, you are ready to develop a plan for marketing to them.

Referral marketing: Hob nob with kindred spirits

Successful lawyers and consultants who have shared their strategies with others say the best tack for good business development is a marketing plan focused on things you like and activities you do well. The self-talk in the preparation phase involves getting some clarity on how choosing a certain avenue to pursue can best align with your personal style.

So how do you pair your interests with networking? Well, if you like running, for example, you could join a running club. Like golf? You could join a golf club, or, you could be in frequent attendance at the local public golf course, and, be ready and open to a foursome. If you're pining for the good old days at college or law school, get active in your alumnae association. It is so much easier to talk to people when you have similar interests. All the while you are doing something you enjoy makes the conversation flow more easily; and, you are making friends and building relationships, which are the cornerstone of business development.

Join relevant professional groups

In addition to the American Bar Association, you can also join professional and trade groups in fields related to your specialty, or at least visit them. You might start out by asking a client or friend who belongs to one of these associations to let you tag along to a meeting. It's well worth the effort. Members of these organizations likely have clients who either now or sometime in the future will need your services. If there a few organizations that capture your interest, you should consider suggesting to you partner, if you have one, that he or she should attend. Your paralegal and or another communicative member of your staff would also be a good bet.

Your law school alumnae association is another great organization on which to set your sights.

It's important to remember these rules of thumb before joining:

- ✓ **Be a one-man or woman band** – Scout out these groups before you commit to membership to make sure you have a lock on the membership seat representing your practice area; you do not want to be one of several attorneys in your field.

- ✓ **Be strategic** – Carefully research the existing membership. Does the membership represent professions who are in your target market, or whose customer base falls within that category? If yes, a membership may be a good investment; if no, set your sights on another group.

These groups also lend themselves to some individualized possibilities for building referrals.

Organize a dinner or event involving a group of your law school classmates, again, taking care that each represents different practice areas. This is a great way to build a referral base.

Host a party, or a happy hour like we do every month or on alternate months. Invite these other attorneys and professionals and ask them to bring along a client or two.

Good people recommend good people and you want to make sure you're on their referral radar. And, don't be afraid to ask: *Do you know anyone who may have need for my services?* When the answer is yes, take names. Also, request that the person who's made the referral give his contact a heads up to say you'll be calling. Then, pick up your phone and make that call.

Give and you will receive

Building a network takes time. Nurturing and maintaining it takes work. When you find an organization you like, join and get involved with it. Volunteering for certain tasks, taking a leadership position and generally being open and accessible to others when they need a recommendation, advice or help establishes you as a trustworthy person who's willing to give as much as receive. And doing what you say you're going to do establishes your credibility. Become known as someone with valuable recommendations, insight and follow-through, and you've built a positive reputation for yourself

Taking your thought leadership public

It's important to gain a reputation as an expert and thought leader in your practice area. There's no better way to do that than to seek out speaking engagements at meetings and events of organizations whose members are likely candidates for your services. For example, if you're a small business owner, your local rotary club may be rife with small business owners who need legal direction, advice and services. If you're an elder care or estate attorney, you may want to arrange speaking engagements at 55 years of age and older communities, or at professional women's groups because women are both savvy investors and typically engaged with the care of their elder parents; getting in front of architects and home contractors and their related affinity groups would be great organizations with which to establish visibility if you're a construction attorney...and the list goes on.

Taking matters online

Your law firm should have a website. And when you get that up and running, you should also consider writing a monthly or quarterly newsletter or a more regularly published blog.

It's up to you to decide whether you prefer short posts or a longer format (there are proponents of each) but whatever your decision, these rules apply:

- ✓ **Be consistent** – Decide when you're going to post or publish (e.g., the day(s) of the week, month, etc.) and how many times a week, a month or a year, if a newsletter. Then stick to it.

- ✓ **Be informative** – Show don't tell. These blogs are not boasts about your accomplishments but rather on topics that educate and inform your audience about issues that affect them. Your knowledge of the subject matter becomes proof of your credentials, and this approach is very much aligned with the concept of you giving as much as you receive.

- ✓ **Be relevant** – Make your content hit home. Make sure you bring up the issues that impact your clients' and prospects' lives and are relevant to your expertise. Your text should be compelling, to help your audience understand in what ways they have specific problems or issues that need attention and inspire them to inquire about your services. When you come across as helpful and knowledgeable, they will likely be calling you.

One other consideration about what you're saying in any of these public forums either in-person or online: Be consistent. Whether you say it, your paralegal says it, your receptionist says it, or the person who performs the very important intake role says it, you must all be on the same page in identifying the unique value proposition that distinguishes your firm.

Reach out and execute

Now that you have some ideas to get you in the marketing and networking mix, you're ready to take things to the next level: outreach. A bunch of names in your contacts data base or business cards in your desk drawer will be for naught if you neglect to reach out and connect. Out of sight, out of mind, so you need an execution plan, and you need to be accountable for executing.

A good plan of attack is to make lists. For example, you could create one list of direct contacts, people you'd met through any of your various networking opportunities, and a second list comprising people to whom your primary sources referred you. Calendar a block of time once a week to call people and follow-through—no cheating—and use that time to make calls.

You should also make certain referral specific notes about each contact. For example, if a person you met at an outing or a meeting, is a wine connoisseur, as part of the conversation you might invite him or her to a wine tasting you'll be attending next week. To someone else you met and agreed that you'd reconnect sometime in the future, you might suggest a date for coffee. To the people on the list of names to whom your primary sources referred you, you might spend the phone time getting to know them better, learning about and listening to what they say about their lives, businesses and potential needs.

Then, follow-up. Send notes, preferably handwritten, thanking them for taking the time to speak; send an article you've read that's relevant to things you discussed in the conversation; or invite them for an in-person lunch or dinner. Once again: Out of sight, out of mind, so it's important to keep your name in front of them. The initial call needs follow-up: the note, the newspaper clip, a link to an article you think they'd like, a specific time to meet over coffee, lunch or dinner or the like. It takes several touchpoints to cultivate the relationship. Plus, following up shows them you are trustworthy and genuinely interested in them.

Just think, if you called six contacts each week—three from your direct referral list and three from your secondary list—you could conceivably call more than 300 people a year. That's not a shabby number for cultivating new business.

Watch your spend

A focus on the importance of your networking relationships cannot detract from the business case. A complementary goal: getting a picture of how much money and time you've spent on networking because that equals cost. You must make certain your efforts are productive and bringing money into the firm. Pay attention to your time and investment in terms of gifts/fees and networking and whether that translated into getting the case, and, if you did, the money you earned on it.

You might be surprised to find that you are spending a lot of money and time courting referral sources that are not giving you the return on investment you want. A referral source that yearly sends you two referrals that will bring in significant revenue for your firm trumps you spending money on a source that sends lots of cases that upon intake review are rejected.

When trying to track networking or marketing, you may be overlooking some important areas. Are you tracking with whom you have coffee, whom you take out for lunch or whom you take out for dinner or drinks? That's networking, and there's money—and time—involved here, too. Consider the expense of Starbucks coffee, or lunch and dinner at nice restaurants, and the time it takes you to get through these events. Your goal is to wrap your arms around how much money and time is spent on networking because when you're tracking billable hours, time spent without a clear reward means you're potentially taking money away from revenue.

Tracking also enables you to see which of your networking activities is working best for you. You may also discover that the marketing efforts of your staff are very effective, or, on the other hand, need to be refined. Even when you're doing everything right, when market conditions change, typically tweaks in your marketing and networking activities will be required. But under no circumstances should they be abandoned because they are vital activities for the growth of your firm. What's more, if you align these responsibilities with interests and past times you like, you may well come to enjoy business development activities after all and derive the benefit of growing your firm.

Chapter To-Do's and Takeaways

Marketing and networking are imperatives for growing your firm.

You can avoid outsourcing marketing to the professionals and keep a lid on costs by strategically developing a referral marketing plan that will foster valuable relationships and allow you to engage in activities you like.

Activities, organizations and events are the forums in which you can meet people.

Public speaking provides a great platform for promoting yourself as a thought leader.

Your online presence is an important complement to your face-to-face referral activities.

You must give to receive.

Everyone in the firm is an ambassador for it; your message must be well-thought out and consistent.

Enjoy your marketing and networking activities and your new relationships, but tracking is important to make sure your efforts are hitting the
bottom line.

CHAPTER 13

Let the Lawyers Practice Law

*Most successful individuals wrongly assume that they can parlay
their success in one field to another, unrelated field. For instance,
where is it written that a good lawyer can successfully run a
business and manage staff? Even if one were capable of practicing
law and managing a business, without a dedicated business
leader on board, the lawyer is often unnecessarily sidetracked
and distracted—thus becoming a less effective attorney.*

-Eric Goldberg, Esq., CELA

You may have learned everything you needed to know about practicing law
in law school. But what may have been missing was teaching you how to
manage your practice.

Granted you paid big bucks for the formal education. But you can't under-cut practice management. It's key to growing your firm, vital to your ability to focus on the practice of law minus distractions and integral to you building a reputation as an attorney who provides superior client service.

Practice management includes the management of legal work, the client relationships and the work of all the firm's professionals who address client needs. When you are managing your practice effectively and efficiently, you are doing the right things right, a la prescient thought leader Peter Drucker, and your outcomes will improve:

✓ You'll be making better and more logical use of firm resources

✓ You'll provide, improved, more efficient, cost-effective service to your clients

✓ You'll experience a more satisfying work experience

✓ You'll see the benefit of these results in your bottom line

Unfortunately, many firms do not operate at this level because their management teams do not have the structure and systems in place to govern a streamlined workflow. Then, too, some attorneys are reticent to embrace any of the new document management technologies.

Poor practice management can send the most impassioned of attorneys into a tailspin, make them feel failed and thwart their desire and their ability to do the level of legal work they were educated to do.

Equally disturbing, poor practice management can lead to costly and ethical mistakes.

A few years ago, an article in *The Atlantic* talked about law firms who remain behind the times in the way they practice law. Traditional law firms have been slow to adapt, says author Lee McMullen Abrahamson,. "Lawyers, she says, are a risk averse bunch."

It is this reticence to adapt to new ways of working and new technologies that lead to some pretty "overt inefficiencies," she says.

From what we can tell from our work with solo practitioners and managing partners in small firms, the same mistakes rear their ugly heads again and again, impeding operations, tarnishing reputations and undercutting the practice of law.

Here are some of the issues that cause problems in small firms.

Improper allocation of staff resources

As a partner, if you're spending your time sorting the mail, answering unscreened phone calls, or occupying yourself with other commoditized administrative work, you are not dividing up responsibilities appropriately among your staff. That non-billable work is important to moving a case to resolution, but when you focus on those tasks, you are taking away from the time you should be spending on high-level legal work, as well as the marketing and business development which are also important requirements for firm growth.

Many lawyers, particularly those in smaller offices, get used to handling these functions, but these are counterproductive work behaviors. It's prudent to delegate nonrevenue tasks to non-billable staff members—especially because, staff members with strong administrative and organizational skill sets, are likely to handle the non-billable work more efficiently than you can—faster and with few, if any, bumps in the road. Put simply, that's just good business: your client comes away satisfied at receiving excellent service; and your employees feel empowered by their individual contributions to a cohesive team and you get to practice law untethered to the busy work that can undermine your productivity.

Org charts and job descriptions

Perhaps you're questioning the necessity of an org chart for your small firm. You may even be reading this and saying to yourself, "That's boring." We'll agree that org charts present the less glamorous part of your law practice, but they are necessary and are the linchpin of proper allocation of staff resources. In fact, without an org chart for your office, you are likely operating your firm within a state of confusion and disorder. And thanks to the chaos, your firm faces the high likelihood of making costly mistakes on a case and spending more time on the completion of non-billable tasks than is necessary. The chaos that results also tends to create a toxic environment for many, if not all, staff members—making your firm a not-so-pleasant place to work, one in which turnover may be high. Plus, the toxicity leads to bad blood; inevitably, time is wasted putting out fires, and this interrupts work focus for everyone involved.

File or case management requires the participation and commitment of the entire staff. Therefore, to address the right tasks (effective tasks) and complete them correctly (efficiently), a task must be defined and identify who will be required to perform it. Particularly in small firms, it is recommended that tasks be evaluated by skill sets as opposed to titles, and be the base of an org chart that is set up accordingly:

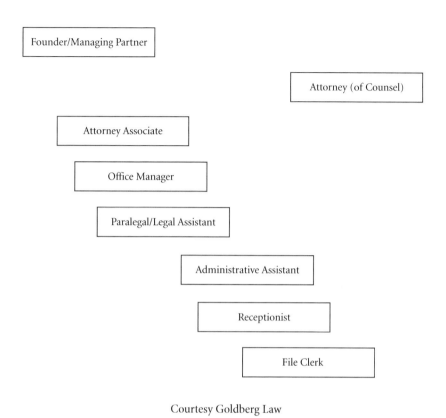

Courtesy Goldberg Law

For example, a person with a welcoming personality and attention to detail might best handle the intake function at the firm; a person with strong organizational and administrative skills and the ability to manage people might best serve as an administrative assistant.

Many levels require decision-making and the leadership skills to direct subordinates. While the leadership and decision-making chain of command must be established in the functional job descriptions, there must always be allowance for feedback on process and task completion at all levels.

Mobility to advance, either by assuming more responsibilities as firm workload and workflow dictate or to move up a level, must be inherent in the organizational structure to incent staff members to perform and grow and to engage them in their work. That said, it is wise to carefully evaluate the skill sets of individual employees and how they align to the functional requirements of a position. For example, the performance of your high producing admin might suffer if you rewarded him or her to a promotion as a legal assistant or offered paralegal training to him or her; it might be a little like asking a dog to behave like a cat.

Training, tools and templates

Instituting a practice management structure reliant on good systems requires your direct input and/or more likely the input of professionals knowledgeable in best practices. We're not just talking theory, principles and clever ideas, but rather a detailed, documented set of guidelines and necessary tools that will take you and your team from start to finish through every phase of the process—and that's right from the get go, from client intake and beyond.

In fact, a consistently weak area surrounds client intake. Oftentimes, employees responsible for intake are using a script or a template that's inadequate. Even worse, they may be operating without a template and script at all. Without sufficient intake, clients whose cases or circumstances don't mesh with your firm slip through the cracks and are passed along to you and an essentially free consultation. You end up spending an hour and a half on the phone doing due diligence and providing a free consult only to discover the prospect is not a good match after all

A well-thought out template that draws out all the necessary information is essential to make the intake process run smoothly. In a best-case scenario, your employee responsible for intake can make an appropriate decision as to whether the client should be passed on to you or an associate attorney as a viable prospect. Alternately, a comprehensive intake form leads to a thorough reporting system that enables you to review the prospect and yeah or nay whether the individual is a fit for your firm.

Time tracking is another area in which you and your staff can run into problems. A template that enables all of you to fill in your hours as well as a template that shows at what points you check in to a project and check out is essential to get a handle on not only your billable hours but the hours your team collectively spends on a case.

Human nature being what it is, there is a tendency for people to delay logging in their hours. Sometimes too, junior attorneys worry that they're spending too much time on the tasks they're assigned and hold off on submitting their hours because they don't want to "look bad." Either scenario can wreak havoc with billing and often in another time-wasting move, requires you to step in to unravel or redo your work on a case.

You can either design your own time-tracking data base to which you mandate everyone submit or purchase one of the time tracking apps that streamlines the process. Also, having a time-tracking database to which everyone has access ramps up transparency in the firm.

Technology a blessing or a curse

There's a general agreement among legal professionals that technology can create more efficient practice management from the ability to integrate smartphone, tablet and mobility use to facilitate anywhere/anytime check-ins with clients to the more sophisticated and expensive document management systems.

Still, there are contrasting views among attorneys about the place of technology in their practices.

Some are attracted by the bright shiny object, the fastest, most powerful systems that some say will greatly increase their bottom lines. Whether these systems will allow them to improve their workflow is largely dependent on whether the attorneys who buy these systems at considerable expense to their firms avail themselves of the training that will enable them and their employees to use the features of the system effectively. Without the proper training, advanced technologies can create more significant stumbling blocks than realizable benefits.

On the other hand, attorneys who for one reason or another are reticent to embrace technology may be slogging along with an old less efficient way of doing things—either using no technology at all or using legacy systems that cannot keep pace with industry updates in compliance and other requirements.

But whether you over-buy or under-utilize, the reality is that you're potentially playing with fire if you avoid increasing your competency in technology. In fact, you could be subjecting yourself to ethics rebuke.

And when we say increasing your competency in technology, we are referencing competency with the *basic software* that attorneys use to practice law. These include case management software, document management software, billing software, email, a PDF system with redacting capabilities and the MS Office Suite, particularly MS Word. Some attorneys may regard these as pedestrian tools, but they address document preparation, drafting and polishing—activities that take up a significant amount of a lawyer's time regardless of his or her practice area. Get comfortable and become proficient with these tools. Used properly, Microsoft work is amazing.

But there's more to the need to embrace technology than time-saving and efficiency. These days attorneys with deficient computer skills are conceivably wasting a client's time and money, and run the risk of getting themselves embroiled in ethical violations. Inefficient use of technology or simply relying on "the old way of doing things" could lead to more billable hours. And these are **unearned** hours, which means an attorney is not serving his or her client fairly.

This is more than just an opinion. Billing fairly to avoid unreasonable fees relates to the ramifications of ABA Model Rule 1.1 which requires lawyers to provide competent representation. What's more, Comment 8 to Model Rule 1.1 now goes further and says, "to maintain the requisite knowledge and skill, a lawyer should keep abreast of changes in the law and its practice including the benefits and risks associated with relevant technology."

Beyond that, in February 2017, the ABA adopted a revised Model Rule for Minimum Continuing Legal Education (MCLE). The modified rule encouraged access to high-quality technology programs by recommending accredited technology MCLE programs that provide education on safe and effective ways to use technology in law practice. "The revised MCLE requirements are important because they reinforce the fact that the duty is continuing and that mere exposure to technology is not enough," says Ivy B. Grey, a senior attorney at Griffin Hamersky in New York City and author of American Legal Style for Perfect IT, a proofreading and editing MS Word add-in for lawyers.

In a May 2017 article in the ABA Journal, Grey highlights Model Rule 1.5 which speaks to the reasonableness of fees. The rule states that a lawyer may not collect unreasonable fees and is ethically obligated to work in a cost-effective manner and to avoid churning hours. She elaborates further: "This means the right person should be performing the work, using the right tools and technology. When a lawyer spends billable time manually performing easily automated tasks or fruitlessly fiddling with MS Word because they haven't learned styles or tracked changes, then that fee is not truly earned. "

Used properly and competently, technology can save you from all the tear your hair out delays and distractions that prevent you from practicing law and from the high risk of ethics violations. Being up to speed on all the areas listed above will put you on a course of productive practice management. And when your practice is managed effectively and efficiently, clients become the recipients of great client service, employees feel valued as contributors to a cohesive team, and you get to practice law and perform the high-level legal work you learned about in law school. Your career and your professional reputation are dependent on this winning combination. So is your firm and all the valued employees who work in it.

Chapter To-Do's and Takeaways

To serve their clients and their employees and to further their careers, lawyers need to practice law and avoid the simpler administrative tasks that can eat up their time and focus and detract from effective, efficient practice management.

Certain mistakes stand out as practice management killers in law firms—particularly small firms—and lead to costly errors in case handling and wasted time.

Allocating staff resources appropriately and within the guidelines of an organizational chart will streamline the process of identifying tasks, delegating responsibilities and make for a pleasing work environment in which employees feel valued and engaged.

A comprehensive intake procedure and template is an important gateway function for turning the right prospects into clients and gets a case off to an efficient start.

Today's technological developments require attorneys to have high technology competency in particularly the basic systems like Microsoft Word; failure to do so can lead to ethical rebuke.

Practice management done right will help you grow your firm, further your career and cultivate an outstanding reputation.

EPILOGUE

There's a revolution going on in the law

Economic and societal conditions have made an impact on many professions, among them the law. Technology and a digital environment have not only connected consumers and workers but also enabled them to create online communities in which they have access to information and the capability to exchange ideas. An entrepreneurial mindset has also caused many workers to strike out on their own, to create businesses and assume thought leadership roles in promoting their insights. These conditions make individuals wiser in their demands for service, urgent in their wants and needs, and fickle when it comes to making the choices that will best solve their problems or accommodate the essentials that dictate where they choose to work.

These 21st century innovations have been both a blessing and a burden for attorneys, especially those in small or solo practitioner firms that lack the financial resources and employee assets of large law practices and corporate legal departments. On the positive side, these advancements provide lawyers with the incredible opportunity to improve their productivity and efficiency to serve their clients more effectively and overall perform in more client-centric ways. In addition, the exposure to new thoughts on effective leadership and the way people should run their businesses provide opportunity for lawyers to deepen their relationships with their employees, further their team's professional development and foster staff engagement and trust.

Still, these changes have come with some cost. Certainly, updating and purchasing the technology to perform faster and more efficiently and of training to remain technologically competent are among these expenses. Also, there is the cost of employee training programs, tuition reimbursement, company retreats, and the restyling of your workspace all which are among the ideas we discuss in this book.

The cost of time is also a consideration: for establishing or updating the founding principles of your firm's vision, mission and values and developing long- and short-term goals that are in alignment with these principles, for streamlining your recruitment processes, improving your ability to delegate and ramping up your communication with your clients and employees.

In *The Law Firm Revolution,* we discuss the pain points attorneys face as they work amid the pressure and competition of today's legal and business environment and the stress they experience from an unending crush of work. We also suggest many of the important ways lawyers can address these issues.

You may decide to pick and choose those areas that you want to address, and for that reason, we have created chapters that serve as standalone guides for a single concern. Or, you may prefer to take some time to complete an entire practice management renovation, and our 13 chapters will give you a comprehensive idea of how to proceed.

We strongly believe that your personal life is a continuum and a reflection of what goes on at work. Therefore, there is a need for these two parts to be in balance for there to be quality in the way you spend time with your colleagues, partners and affiliates, and, not least of all, with your family and friends. Whatever your objective, we hope you will enjoy reading *The Law Firm Revolution* and find it a helpful resource to enrich your practice and your life.

Clelia Pergola
Barbara Mannino

BIBLIOGRAPHY

Abrahamson, Lee McMullen "Why Are So Many Law Firms Trapped in 1995?" *The Atlantic*,
October 1, 2015. https://www.theatlantic.com/business/archive/2015/10/why-are-so-many- law-firms-trapped-in-1995/408319/.

Adams, A. J., MAPP. "Seeing is Believing. The Power of Visualization." *Psychology Today*.
December 3, 2009. https://www.psychologytoday.com/blog/flourish/200912/seeing-is-believing-the-power-visualization.

"Articulating Vision, Mission, and Values." Students at the Center Hub.
https://studentsatthecenterhub.org/toolkit/articulating-vision-mission-and-values/.

Bulyago, Zach. "Inside Google's Culture of Success and Employee Happiness."
Kissmetrics Blog. San Francisco, 2013.
https://blog.kissmetrics.com/googles-culture-of-success/.

Cleek, Matthew. Funding Sage. "Clarify the Vision – 10 Questions to create an effective vision statement." April 12, 2016.
http://fundingsage.com/clarify-the-vision-10-questions-to-create-an-effective-vision-statement/.

"Client Lawyer Relationships. Rule 1.5. Fees. American Bar Association. Center for Professional Responsibility. March 2017.
https://www.americanbar.org/groups/professional_responsibility/publications/model_rules_of_professional_conduct/rule_1_5_fees.html.

Coleman, Alison. "Is Google's model of the creative workplace the future of the office?" *the guardian.com*. June 28, 2017. https://www.theguardian.com/careers/2016/feb/11/is-googles-model-of-the-creative-workplace-the-future-of-the-office.

"Comment on Model Rule 1.1." American Bar Association, Center for Professional Responsibility. March 2017. https://www.americanbar.org/groups/professional_responsibility/publications/model_rules_of_professional_conduct/rule_1_1_competence/comment_on_rule_1_1.html.

Davis, Jenny B. "Designing Your Office Space to Save Money and Boost Productivity—Without Sacrificing Style." ABA Journal. July 1, 2014. http://www.abajournal.com/magazine/article/designing_your_law_office_to_save_money_and_boost_productivity.

DeMers, Jayson, AudienceBloom. "7 Strategies for Delegating Better and Getting More Done." *Inc.* May 7, 2015. https://www.inc.com/jayson-demers/7-strategies-to-delegate-better-and-get-more-done.html.

Dimka, Dennis. "5 Reasons Every Lawyer Needs One Note." Uptime LegalWorks. January 12, 2017. https://uptimelegalworkscom/2017/01/12/5-reasons-every-lawyer-needs-onenote/.

Dimka, Dennis. "11 Reasons Your Law Firm Needs a Document Management System." Uptime LegalWorks. February 28, 2015. https://uptimelegalworks.com/2015/02/28/11-reasons-your-law-firm-needs-document-management/.

"DISC Insights." The Institute for Motivational Living. PeopleKeys. Youngstown,Ohio.
https://www.discinsights.com/disc-theory#.WZs1Cq2ZMdU.

Entrepreneur Media, Inc. Staff. "10 Questions to Answer When Writing Your Mission Statement." *entrepreneur.com*. February 3, 2015.
https://www.entrepreneur.com/article/241954.

"Explaining the Technology Behind Matter Centricity." *Findlaw*. Thomson Reuters. New York. June 1, 2017.
http://technology.findlaw.com/legal-software/explaining-the-technology-behind-matter-centricity.html.

Frost, Peter. "Why Compassion Counts! Journal of Management Inquiry 20, no. 4 December 2011. 395-401] [first published June 1, 1999]

Fallon, Nicole. "SWOT Analysis: What Is It and When to Use It." *Business News Daily*. March 28. 2017.
http://www.businessnewsdaily.com/4245-swot-analysis.html.

Gallo, Amy. "Why Aren't You Delegating?" Harvard Business Review. Boston, July 26, 2012.
https://hbr.org/2012/07/why-arent-you-delegating.

Gensler U.S. Workplace Survey 2016.
https://www.gensler.com/news/press-releases/us-workplace-survey-2016-findings.

Gensler U.S. Workplace Survey 2013.
https://www.gensler.com/research-insight/research/the-2013-us-workplace-survey-1.

Gerber, Michael E. The EMyth Revisited. New York: Harper Business. 1995.

Goodman, Joanna. "Expert Opinion 4: Measuring Internal communication in professional services firms." Sinicom.
http://www.sinicom.com/Sub%20Pages/pubs/articles/article94.pdf.

Grey, Ivy B., "Not Competent in Basic Tech? You Could Be Overbilling Your Clients and Be on Shaky Ground." *Legal Rebels*, American Bar Association, May 15, 2017.
http://www.abajournal.com/legalrebels/article/
tech_competence_and_ethical_billing.

Hammond, Michael, Powers, Mark. "The Firm: Long-term marketing goals, short-term planning." *Detroit Legal News.* May 10, 2013
http://www.legalnews.com/detroit/1375868.

Hoover, Amy via Jacqueline Smith. "17 Ways to Be Indispensable at Work." *Forbes Online,* Sept 5, 2013.
https://www.forbes.com/sites/jacquelynsmith/2013/09/05/17-ways-to-be-indispensable-at-work/#723e83bf274d.

Hurt, Karin, Dye, David. *Winning Well: A Manager's Guide to Getting Results Without Losing Your Soul.* New York: Amacom, 2016.

"Improving Business Processes: Streamlining Tasks to Improve Efficiency." Mind Tools.
https://www.mindtools.com/pages/article/improving-business-processes.htm.

"Inside Google workplaces, from perks to nap pods," cbsnews.com. 2013
https://www.cbsnews.com/news/
inside-google-workplaces-from-perks-to-nap-pods/.

Jones, David P. *The Million Dollar Hire: Build Your Bottom Line One Employee at a Time.* San Francisco: Jossey-Bass. 2011.

LaCivita, Andrew. *The Hiring Prophecies: Psychology Behind Recruiting Successful Employees.* Bloomington, IN: Balboa Press, 2015.

Mannino, Barbara. "How to Stay Productive When No One Else Is." Fox Business. December 30, 2013.
http://www.foxbusiness.com/features/2013/12/30/how-to-stay-productive-when-no-one-else-is.html.

"Mission & Vision Statements: What is the Difference Between Mission, Vision and Values Statements?" Society for Human Resource Management (SHRM). December 20, 2012.
https://www.shrm.org/search/pages/default.aspx.

McCaffrey, Margaret. "Building Word of Mouth Referrals." *Slaw.* June 9, 2017.
http://www.slaw.ca/2017/06/09/building-word-of-mouth-referrals/.

McCaffrey, Margaret. "Marketing Strategy II: Do You Know Where Your Clients Are?" *Slaw.* April 4, 2017
http://www.slaw.ca/2017/04/07marketing-strategy-ii-do-you-know-where-your-clients-are/.

McChesney, Chris, Huling, Jim, Covey, Sean. "How to Set Wildly Important Business Goals, and What They'll Do for You." *Fast Company.* April 24, 2012.
https://www.fastcompany.com/1835210/how-set-wildly-important-goals-and-what-theyll-do-you.

Nawaz, Sabina. "For Delegation to Work, It Has to Come With Coaching." Harvard Business Review. Boston, May 5, 2016.
https://hbr.org/2016/05/for-delegation-to-work-it-has-to-come-with-coaching.

Owen, Mark J. "Why team members should not be indispensable." http://www.markjowen.com/no-team-member-is-indispensable/.

Pergola, Clelia. The Inbox Theory" Fairfield, NJ. 2016.

Pergola, Clelia. The Outbox Theory^T. Fairfield, NJ. 2016.

Rosenberg, Merrick, Silvert, Daniel. *Taking Flight!:Master the DISC Styles to Transform Your Career, Your Relationships...Your Life / Edition 1.* Upper Saddle River, NJ: FT Press, 2015.

Rowe, Tom. "Law Firm Reporting is More Than Financial Reporting," OTB Consulting. Cary NC. May 2015.

Ryan, Matt. White Paper, "Case Management: Why Doesn't Every Law Firm Use It? Criteria for Use, Success and Failure." Legal Files. (Springfield Ill) http://www.legalfiles.com/Portals/0/whitepages/Case-Management-for-Law-Firms.pdf.

Schneider, Michael. "Google Employees Weighed In on What Makes a Highly Effective Manager. Technical Expertise Came in Dead Last." *Inc.* July 2, 2017. https://www.inc.com/michael-schneider/google-did-an-internal-study-that-will-forever-change-how-they-hire-and-promote-.html.

Slovic, Susan. "How to make a vision board for your business and why you should." The Small Business Expert blog. March 3, 2016. http://www.susansolovic.com/2016/03/how-to-make-a-vision-board-for-your-business-and-why-you-should/.

Stewart, James. "Looking for a Lesson in Google's Perks." *The New York Times*. (New York, March 15, 2013). http://www.nytimes.

com/2013/03/16/business/at-google-a-place-to-work-and-play.
html?mcubz=1.

Smith, E.E. "Are You Left- or Right-Brain Dominant?" *Psychology Today.*
Oct 19, 2012.
https://www.psychologytoday.com/blog/not-born-yesterday/201210/
are-you-left-or-right-brain-dominant.

Stack, Laura. *Right Things Right: How the Effective Executive Spends Time.*
Oakland, CA. Berrett-Koehler Publishers, Inc. 2015.

Strong, Frank. "5 Essential Practice Management Reports for Small Law
Firms." Lexis Nexis Business of Law Blog January 12, 2015. http://busines-
soflawblog.com/2015/01/practice-management-reports/.

"The Google Way of Motivating Employees." cleverism.com (Sept 25
2014).
https://www.cleverism.com/google-way-motivating-employees/.

"The Roles of Vision, Mission and Values."
https://open.lib.umn.edu/principlesmanagement/
chapter/4-3-the-roles-of-mission-vision-and-values/

The Ultimate Guide to Conducting a SWOT Analysis. BPlans.

Vaughan, Ken. "From Mission to Action." New Horizon Partners.
September 5, 2016.
http://newhorizonpartners.com/the-funnel-from-mission-to-action/

Ward, Susan. "10 Goal Setting Tips for Setting Goals You Will Achieve."
"The balance." July 27. 2016.
https://www.thebalance.com/goal-setting-tips-2948134.

Ward, Stephanie Francis. "50 simple ways you can market your practice." ABA Journal. July 1, 2013.
http://www.abajournal.com/magazine
article/50_simple_ways_you_can_market_your_practice.

"What is Disc? Personality Profiling That's Quick, Simple and Effective," DISCUS Axiom Internet Group Limited Manchester United Kingdom.
https://www.discusonline.com/disc/what-is-disc.php.

Whitten, Neal, PMP. "10 Traits of the Indispensable Team Member."
https://www.projecttimes.com/articles/10-traits-of-the-indispensable-team-member.html.

Worline, Monica C., Dutton, Jane E. *Awakening Compassion at Work: The Quiet Power That Elevates People and Organizations.* Oakland, CA: 2017.

Zhang, Haiyan. "How Do I Recognize Thee? Let Me Count the Ways, IBM Smarter Workforce Institute. July 2015.
https://www-01.ibm.com/common/ssi/cgi-bin
ssialias?htmlfid=LOW14298USEN.

Zavieh, Megan. "Keeping Better Notes." Daily Dispatch, Attorney at Work. January 26, 2015.
https://www.attorneyatwork.com/keeping-better-notes/.